SOCIAL ANTHROPOLOGY

SOCIAL ANTHROPOLOGY

By

Dr. S. Narayan

GYAN

Social Anthropology

ISBN : 978-81-212-0234-3

First Published 1988, reprint 2013 in India by
Gyan Publishing House
23, Main Ansari Road, Daryaganj,
New Delhi - 110002
Phones : 23282060, 23261060
Fax : (011) 23285914
E-mail: books@gyanbooks.com
website: gyanbooks.com

Printed at : Sagar Color Scan, New Delhi.

PREFACE

This work of mine is a long delayed exercise and has an interesting beginning. Anthropology in India has a long and chequered history. The British, American and Indian anthropologists worked on different dimensions of Man in India. A good number of research reports and ethnographic studies are published each year, but the students of Man in totality in India still feel a gap in their knowledge. Such gap was bridged to a great extent by Shri D.N. Majumdar and Shri T.N. Madan by their textbooks. Later on Sarwashri Vidyarthi, Mathur and Singh also tried to bridge the gap by providing their works in Hindi.

Later on sporadic attempts were made but nothing significant come out. It so happened that in 1973-74, I did some spade work for a text book in social anthropology as at that time I was in the P.G. Department of Anthropology in Ranchi University. Later on I shifted to Space Application Centre, Ahmedabad and the work remained at a rudimentry level.

It was in 1981 that I got associated with UPSC for teaching and examination. For this I had to go through books and journals. So, since 1981 till to date I remained engaged with this project of mine and ultimately the result of the project is with you. To me it appears good and uptodate though there might be some mistakes. I will appreciate if such mistakes are pointed out to me so as to enable me to rectify them in the next edition.

I am specially thankful to those students who were regularly coming to me with their questions. Their constant questioning also perked me in completing this work. I am specially thankful to my mother Mrs. Shakuntala Devi and to my wife Mrs. Sobha Narayan and to our children, Shiwani, Subhash and Savidhi who took care of my comfort while I was working on this book. I have also received assistance from Shri Dhirendra Narayan, Shri Satyendra Narayan, Shri Vijay Kumar Sinha and wish to put it on record. I am also thankful to Shir. M.J. Philip, the typist of our Institute who always took pains in reading my little dirty handwriting with great interest. I am also thankful to Dr. S.F. Rub and Shri Prabhash Prasad Singh, the Deputy and the Asstt. Librarian of our Institute, for their help extended to me in completing this work.

A.N. Sinha Institute of
Social Studies
Patna

SACHINDRA NARAYAN

CONTENTS

1

INTRODUCTION

INTRODUCTION

History has no beginning nor has anthropology. But historians of anthropology have to start somewhere. There is a great temptation, to say, that anthropology 'begins' with Tylor or Helveitius or Aristotle. The beginning of anthropology is very *like the beginning of mankind itself—the only way to* deal with such an ill considered question is to create false entities and make declarations by scholarly fiat. There is no event, no person, before which there was no anthropology and after which there was. Rather, there are human curiosities and activities that we today think of as anthropological and we extend our conceptualization into the past, to periods before the word was even coined, and certainly to periods when the word meant something very different from what we mean by it today.

Aristotle is said to have coined the term anthropologist meaning by it the gossip who talks about himself. The 18th century German idealist thinker Kant wrote a book entitled Anthropology in 1789 suggesting the animal origin of man. The word had already found its way into English : an anonymous book published in 1655, entitled Anthropologic Abstracted, defined anthropology as the history of human soul and human anatomy. The word was incorporated in the British encyclopaedia by 1822, however, without gaining in clarity of meaning. It is defined therein as a discourse upon human nature.

Anthropology is derived from the root words Anthropos—meaning man—and Logos—meaning science. This etymological meaning is a sufficient, accurate definition of the scope of the subject. As Kluckhon has pointed out, out of all the sciences which study various aspects of man, anthropology is the one which comes nearest to being a total study of man. To give expression to the fact that an anthropologist studies all that can possibly be studied about man, some anthropologists have said that anthropology is the science of man without portfolio. And this vast study is limited neither by time nor by space nor even, as is erroneously supposed by some, by the cultural level of a human society. Anthropology studies man present as also past and also his sub-human and pre-human origins, it studies man on any part of the earth ; and it studies man irrespective of whatever he is—savage or civilized. But it must not be presumed that by the study of man is implied the study of human anatomy, human evolution, human growth and genetics only. The study of man also includes the study of man's feeling, thinking and action-patterns. To borrow the title of Herskovite's well known book on anthropology, anthropology is the study of Man and His Works.

To define anthropology in terms of its interest in man is admittedly to be less than explicit, for according to this definition anthropology would appear to encompass a whole catalogue of disciplines—Sociology, Psychology, Political Science, Economics, History, Human Biology and perhaps even the humanistic disciplines of philosophy and literature. Needless to say, the many other disciplines concerned with man would not be happy to be relegated to sub-branches of anthropology (After all, most of them have been separate disciplines longer than anthropology, and they consider their jurisdcitions to be some what distinctive). There must, then, be something unique about anthropology—a reason for having developed as a separate discipline and for having retained a separate identity over the hundred or so years since its inception.

Scope

One typically envisions anthropologists as travelling to unkown corners of the world to study exotic peoples or digging far into the earth to uncover the fossil remains or the tools and pots of men who lived so long ago, that it troubles the imagination. These views, though clearly stereotyped, do indicate one way in which anthropology differs from other disciplines concerned with man ; anthropology is broader in scope. It is explicitly and directly concerned with all varieties of man and it considers man of all periods, beginning with the emergence of man over a million years ago and tracing his development until the present. Thus, anthropologists attempt to broaden the study of man by being both comparative and historical on a world wide basis. Every part of the world that has ever had a human population is of interest to anthropologists.

True anthropologists have not always been as broad and comprehensive in their concerns as they are today ; traditionally they have left the study of Western civilization and similarly complex societies and their recorded histories, to other disciplines. In recent years, however, this general division of labour among the disciplines has begun to disappear. Now, anthropologists can be found at work in primitive villages as well as in cities of the industrial world.

One might wonder what induces the anthropologist to choose so broad a subject for study. In part he is motivated by the feeling that any generalization we entertain about man (and consequently about ourselves) should be shown to be applicable to many different times and places of human existence. In this way, we can avoid believing things about man that are applicable only in a particular setting. For example, before Margret Mead embarked on her famous field study of Samoa (which was later reported in her Coming Age in Samao, 1928) many Americans believed that adolescence was necessarily a period of 'storm and stress' due to psychological changes that occur at puberty. However, on the basis of her observations of Samoan adolescents, who did not seem to show signs of emotional upheavals Mead concluded that Western belief about adolescence was to some extent a function of the way that growing up is managed in Western Societies. Anthropologists, then are often in a position to illuminate beliefs and practices generally accepted by their contemporariess, for they are acquainted with human life in an unusual variety of geographical and historical settings.

Not only are anthropologists concerned with universality of

human beliefs and customs; they are also interested in exploring the possible universality of biological traits. In our own society, for example, children are constantly told to drink milk because it will make them strong and healthy, yet anthropologists have known for years that in many parts of the world where cows and goats are kept, people do not drink fresh milk. For such people, drinking fresh milk would usually cause sickness. So, in some places, people sour their milk to make it digestable ; or else they do not drink milk at all. Human populations, then, vary in their biological characteristics ;what is healthy for some is not necessarily healthy for all.

The Holistic Approach

Another distinguishing feature of anthropology is its holistic approach to man ; not only do anthropologists study all varieties of man, they also study all aspects of man's experience. For example, in writing a description of a group of people, an anthropologist might include a section on the history of the area, the environment, organizations of family life, settlement pattern, political and economic systems, religion, styles of art and dress, general features of language and so on.

In the past the holistic approach was exhibited by most individual anthropologists. Today, as in many other disciplines, there is a tendency toward specialization in investigations as a function of increasing knowledge. Thus, one anthropologist studies the physical characteristics of man's prehistoric ancestors, another the biological effect of the environment on a human population overtime, and still another the interrelationships of cultural factors. Even though same anthropologists may choose to specialize in a branch or sub-branch of the field, the discipline of anthropology retains its holistic orientation in that its speciality areas, taken together, describe many aspects of human exisence, past and present on all levels of complexity.

Distinctiveness

If anthropology differs in scope and approach from other disciplines concerned with man, it also differs somewhat in interests. Anthropologists are concerned with many types of questions : where, when and why did people first begin living in cities ? Why do some people have darker skin than others ? Why do some languages have more colour terms than other languages ? Why are men in some societies allowed to be married to more than one wife simultaneously ? Although these questions seem to deal with very different aspects of human existence, they do have at least one thing in common. They all deal with a typical characteristic that is shared by some particular human population.

The typical characteristic might be relatively dark sin, or a language having many colour terms or the practice of marrying several wives ; in fact, it could be almost any human trait or custom. The population studied is most often a single society that is, a population occupying a particular territory and speaking a common language. At times, however, the population studied by Anthropologists may be larger or smaller than a single society—that is a population occupying a particular territory and speaking a common language. In short, the anthropologists is usually concerned with describing how and explaining why human populations are different or similar with respect to certain distinctive characteristics.

Branches

With the inclusion of a body of generalizations on application, anthropology may be conveniently divided into :

1. *Physical anthropology* or the study of human evolution and growth.
2. *Prehistory and cultural anthropology* or the study of the works of man, broadly known as Social Anthropology in India.
3. *Archaeology*
4. *Anthropological Linguistics*
5. *Ethnology* or the racial and cultural distribution of man
6. *Applied Anthropology.*
7. *Action Anthropology.*
8. *Urgent Anthropology.*

1. **Physical Anthropology**

Physical Anthropology studies man as an evolving physical

organism and determines how and why human populations differ physically. The distinctive questions of physical anthropology are (a) questions about the emergence of man and his evolution (an area of physical anthropology called human palaeontology and (b) questions about how and why contemporary man varies biologically (an area referred to as human variation).

In order to reconstruct the emergence and evolution of man, human palaeontologists search for and study fossils, the buried, hardened remains of humans and prehumans. Palaeontologists working in East Africa, for example, have excavated the fossil remains of man like creatures who lived more than 2 million years ago ; their findings have helped physical anthropology to approximate when prehistoric man acquired upright posture, flexible hands and a larger brain. To understand the evolutionary sequence, the human palaeontologists may make use not only of the fossil record but of geological information on the succession of climates, environments and plant and animal populations. Moreover, the reconstruction of man's past is accompanied by an interest in the behaviour and evolution of man's closest relatives among the mammals, the apes and monkeys who like himself are members of the order of primates. Species of primates are observed in the field and the laboratory, especially popular is the chimpanzee, who bears a close resemblance to humans in behaviour and physical appearance, has similar blood types and is susceptible to many of the same diseases. From primate studies, the physical anthropologoist seeks to distinguish those characteristics that are distinctly human from those that might be part of a generalized primate heritage. In this way we might be able to guess what the prehistoric ancestors of man were like, for if all living primates (including) man share a certain characteristic, that characteristic was probably found in the first prehuman forms from which modern man evolved. The inferences from such studies are checked against the fossil record. Thus, the evidence from the earth, collected in bits and pieces, is correlated with scientific observations of our closest living relatives.

In short, physical anthropologists who are interested in the evolution of man are like detectives in that they piece together bits of information from a number of different sources, construct theories accounting for the change observed in the fossil record, and attempt to evaluate these theories by cross checking one kind of evidence against another. Human palaeontology thus overlaps a great deal with other disciplines such as geology, general vertebrate (and particularly private) palaeontology, comparative anatomy and the study of comparative private behaviour.

The second major area of physical anthropology— the study of human variation—discusses how and why do the contemporary human populations differ in physical or biological characteristics. All living peoples belong to one species—*Homosapiens*—for all can successfully interbreed. Yet there is much that varies among human populations. In order to understand the kinds of biological variation observable in contemporary human populations, physical anthropologists employ principles, concepts and techniques of human genetics (the study of how traits are inherited in man), population biology (the study of environmental effects on and interaction with population characte ristics) and epidemology (the study of how and why diseases differentially affect different populations). Researches in human variation, therefore, overlaps with research in other fields. Those who call themselves physical anthropologists, however, are most centrally concerned with human populations and how they vary biologically.

Another kind of question, always of interest to physical anthropologists and now of growing general concern, asks how human populations have adapted physically to their environmental conditions. Speculation has led anthropologists to diverse areas of the earth. They have found answers that make us hopeful that human beings may adjust, in time, even to industrial pollution and the other noxious wastes that are continually altering our environment, for anthropologists have shown us that the bodies of men in other times and other places, have often adapted to environmental conditions that threatened human life.

2. Pre-histion and Cultural Anthropology

To an anthropologists, the term "culture" generally refers to the customary ways of thinking and behaving that are characteristic of a particular population or society. Culture, therefore, is composed of such things as language, knowledge, laws, religious beliefs, food preferences, music, workhabits, taboos and so forth.

In everyday usage the word "culture" refers to a desirable quality that we may acquire by attending a sufficient number of plays and dance concerts and trudging through several miles of art gallaries. The anthropologist, however, has a different definition. In the following extract, Ralph Linton makes clear how the layman's definition of 'culture' differs from that of the anthropologist.

"It refers to the total way of life of any society, not simply to those parts of this way which the society regards as higher or more desirable. Thus culture, when applied to our own ways of life, has nothing to do with playing the piano or reading Browning. For the social scientist such activities are simply elements within the totality of our culture. This totality also includes such mundane activities as washing dishes or driving an automobile, and for the purposes of cultural studies these stand quite on a par with "the finer things of life". It follows that for the social scientist there are no uncultured societies or even individuals. Every society has a culture, no matter how simple this culture may be and every human being is cultured, in the sense of participating in some culture or other (Ralph Linton, The Cultural Background of Personality, New York : Appleton—Century Crofts, p. 30).

3. **Archaeology**

The archaeologist seeks not only to reconstruct the daily life and customs of prehistoric peoples, but also to trace cultural change and offer possible explanations as to why those changes occurred. His concern is similar to the historians but he reaches much farther back in time. The historian deals only with cultures possessing written records, limiting himself, therefore, to the last 5,000 years of human history. For all past cultures lacking a written record and this includes many cultures within the past 5000 years which did not develop writing, the archaeologist serves as historian. Lacking written records for study he is completed to reconstruct history from the remains of human cultures he finds. Some of them as grandiose as the Mayan temples discovered at Chichen Itza in Yucatah, Mexico, but more often as ordinary as bits of broken pottery, stone tools, and even garbage heaps. Such like remains enable the archaeologists to recreate a history for human societies that left no other records behind them.

The archaeologist works in diverse areas of the world, for remains of past cultures have been discovered on every continent. One fruitful location for prehistoric data has been France, where Neandarthal cultures left extraordinary records on the walls of caves and in the soil. Archaeology has two major concerns. One is to establish the sequences of cultural development (how ways of life have changed) in different parts of the world. The second major concern of archaeology is to understand why certain changes took place when and where.

4. Anthropological Linguistics

Another branch of cultural anthropology is Linguistics, the study of languages. As a science, the study of language is somewhat older than anthropology. The two disciplines became closely associated in the early days of anthropological field work, when anthropologists enlisted the help of linguists to learn primitive languges. When it became increasingly evident that language plays a basic role in the development of human culture—language, after all, is the primary means by which customs are transmitted from generation to generation —anthropology became more reliant on linguistics. In contrast to other linguists, however, anthropological linguists are most interested in the history and structure of unwritten language. This focus requires a more extensive array of techniques of analysis and investigation than those used by earlier linguists.

Like the physical anthropologist, the linguist is interested in changes that have taken place over time, as well as in contemporary variation. Thus, anthropological linguists are concerned with the emergence of language and how languages diverge over centuries ; this aspect of linguistics is known as comparative or historical linguistics. They are also interested in how contemporary languages differ specially in regard to how they are constructed and used.

This area of linguistics is generally called description linguistics. More specially, the study of how languages are constructed is called structural linguistics, while the study of how language is used in actual speech is called sociolinguistics or ethnolinguistics.

5. Ethnology

The ethnologist attempts to understand how and why peoples today, and in the recent past, differ in their customary ways of thinking and acting. In other words, ethnology is concerned with patterns of behaviour such as marriage customs kinship organization, political and economic systems, religion, folklore, arts and music—and how those differ in contemporary societies. The ethnologist also studies in dynamics of culture—how cultures develop and change and how they interact with other cultures—as well as the interaction of diverse beliefs and practices within a culture and their effect on individual personality. Thus the aim of the ethnologist is largely the same as that of the archaeologist. However, the enthnologist uses data which are collected first hand by field workers, whereas the archaeologist must work with fragmentary remains of past cultures, on the basis of which he can only make educated guesses about the actual customs of prehistoric peoples. One type of ethnologist, the ethnographer, usually spends a year or so living with talking to and observing the people whose customs he wants to study. His work in the field often results in a detailed description (an ethnography) of many aspects of customary behaviour and thought of those people. The ethnographer not only describes general patterns of life but also may ask such questions as : How are economic and political behaviour related ? How many customs of people he adopted to environmental conditions ? Is there any relationship between beliefs about the supernatural and beliefs or practices in the natural world ? In other words, the ethnographer describes the ways of life of a particular groupof people and may also suggest explanations for some of the customs he has observed.

6. Applied Anthropology

When the knowledge of anthropology is applied for the welfare and development of mankind it becomes applied anthropology. It is the application of the findings of physical and cultural anthropologists in ordering race and industrial relations ; in colonial administration ; in development programmes of developing countring and so on.

7. Action Anthropology

When the knowledge of anthropology is not only applied but is brought into action for the development of mankind it becomes action anthropology. The trained anthropologists with their anthropological expertise experiments development designs for the welfare and development of the human population.

8. Urgent Anthropology

The anthropological problems taken up on priority basis with anthropological techniques and expertise are the subject matter of urgent anthropology.

To sum up, anthropology is no longer a vague study, nor even ambitiously vague as a study without a portfolio. Anthropology is a well defined study of the physical, social and cultural aspects of man. Anthropology is not idlers pursuit, or a study that does not concer us very vitally in our own lives. It is not a study of exotic savage and supposedly funny, queer customs only, it is not the academic digging up of the past, of broken pottery and fossilized skulls and bones. It is all these and much more; it is all these with an aim and aim is as Evans—Pritchard puts it, to have an understanding of the wondrous creature that is man, wherever and whatever time past or present, he has lived or lives today. The immediate relevancy of anthropology to modern life has been summed up by Kluckhen when he compares anthropology to a mirror into which man, without any labels of primitive or civilised may look to understand and appreciate his own unbounded physical and cultural variety.

2

MARRIAGE

Sex as an organising factor—Definition

Forms of Marriage

Ways of Acquiring Mates

Premarital and Extramarital Relations

Divorce

History of Marriage

MARRIAGE

Sex as an Organising Factor

The basic anatomical and physiological differences of sex are happily obvious. A limited number of sex associated characteristics also appear to be transmitted at the genetic level, such as are apparent tendency shared with many other animals for dominance and passivity in the male and female, respectively, possibly universal tendencies to greater hardiness among females in infancy and old age and certain sex linked traits such as the dominance or recessivity of colour blindness which are under genetic and medical scrutiny.

At the level of customs, the comparative view of anthropology is that almost any cultural behaviour assigned to females in one culture may be found assigned to males in some other culture. Basketry or pottery making is a male occupation in our culture but a female occupation in another. Religious leadership may be strongly assigned to men or alternatively to women. Margaret Mead gives vivid illustration of such differences in her book MALE AND FEMALE (1949). She has pointed out that even baby suckling can be passed over to a modern husband by way of a feeding bottle. The anthropologist, however, does discuss some high frequency tendencies in man's overall behaviour relating to sex differences.

In every group the physiological differences between males and females, and the mating and the procreative drive are constants, entering deeply into socio-cultural patterns. The sex factor cuts every society approximately into two halves.

This phase of life is inescapable—even if we wanted to escape. Each society has its own more or less unique systems of relationship between males and females, between females and females and between males and males. Differing cluster of beliefs, values and sentiments surround the matter of sex, sometimes placing one sex as superior to the other, sometimes excluding one or the other sex from certain spheres of activity such as religious ceremonial or political leadership, and always providing a body of prescriptions and proscriptions (do's and don'ts) to regulate the consorting of males and females and the business of procreation. Sex is always a subject of high interest, and is likely to be dramatized and surrounded with tension and sentiment. It is obviously associated with group continuity, yet has in it dangerous and complicating possibilities of disrupting other valued social relations.

The pairing of persons of opposite sex during the reproduction age period, particularly in mating, tends always to be narrowly channeled by stringent rules and sanctions. It is a complete misreading of anthropological data to consider so-called primitives as a whole to be very free in sex relations, or to postulate early man to have had anything like the 'promiscuity' which some ninteenth century theorists propounded.

BOGARDUS—"Marriage is an institution admitting according to men and women to family life, that is, to living in the institute personal relationships of husband and wife for the primary purpose of begetting and rearing children. This institution has social approbation and religions sanction".

Marriage has been defined as follows in the Dictionary of Sociology :

"The social institution that provides the recognized form for entering into matrimony or setting up a family unit. (Encylopaedia Britanica Vol. 14, p. 184) definesit as it is the combina tion of mating with parenthood which constitutes marriage in higher animals including man.

WESTERMARCK—"Marriage is rooted in the family ather than the family in marriage".

To conclude marriage is a socially accepted and recognised permanent sexual relationship between a male and a female for the purpoed of procreation, for the continuity of a family and civilization at large.

Every human group apparently has some form of marriage in the sense of a public or legal recognition of a more enduring pair relationship and responsibility. A couple may never have seen each other before (Indian examples) or they may have been busy for sometime with a 'courtship' or again they may have been living together for a long period and there may even be one or more children from the union. The actual wedding may be a highly formalized affair with high religious or other ceremonies, feasting and passing of wealth ; at the other extreme, it may be by our ideas virtually non-existent as where a pair of lovers in some Melanesian groups deliberately allow others to steal a book at them so that parents and community can see them consorting openly and so take cognizance of their association. The essential points are that this union has social recognition and sanction, and the "bride" and "groom" publicly acknowledge the obligations that the particular society prescribes for married status.

Some theorists have considered the marital association to have originated from the need for channeling the physiological sex drive, and this is a significant function in many marriage systems in the sense of limiting competition for sexual privilege as well as defining responsibility for its consequences. Anthropologists generally consider that the prime function of the stablized marriage union is to provide a secure setting in which children can be socially identified, nurtured or and brought to mature status. This ordinarily involves responsible participation by both a female and a male as the parties who will acknowledge "parenthood" and will bear the brunt of child care. In this connection we can note that all societies distinguish more or less between legitimate and illegitimate children—though the latter are accepted by some societies with much less discrimination than by others.

Marriages may also consummate additional functions from society to society.

Notably it channels the handling of property.

It provides an intimate "home" group for eating, sleeping working and relaxing together.

Marriage in most groups symbolises attainment of adult status. Each union links together a more or less extensive group of people—the kinsmen and friends of the groom—into some new relationship and interaction, which is the main reason why in nearly all societies parents, relatives and acquaintances of young persons have a large say, and in some groups the dominant say, in choosing their partners.

All societies have more or less institutionalized a set of rules governing the selection of spouses.

Among all peoples marriage is forbidden within some well defined "incest group"

Marriage ensures a biological satisfaction (that of sex) and a psychological satisfaction (that of having children) on the individual plane, on the wider collective plane, it ensures a two-fold survival, viz. that of the group and its culture.

Forms of Marriage

Marriage in tribal India as also in other parts of the country and world is of several types. We find rules laying down prohibitions, performances and prescriptions in deciding the form of marriage.

Preferences and Prohibitions

A taboo on sexual relations between closely related kin like parents and children and between siblings is universal. An extension of this 'nuclear prohibition' is found everywhere including among the castes and tribes of India.

Since the practice of marrying outside the family is found extended to wider groups like clans, as among the Gonds, Baigas, Hos, Korwas, Oraons, Khoshi, Nagas etc. The conclusion is that rules of incest cannot have a biological implication, viz., the ban on inbreeding due to the fear that it may lead to racial degeneration. Psychological disorders being the effect rather than the cause of incest also do not bear a full suritiny. The cultural factor of widening the area of co-operation, social contact may be considerably responsible for this prohibition on sex relations between close relatives. Breaches of the rule are often punished met with heavy fines and even communication of the offender. The fear of supernatural punishment in case of the violation of the rule of marrying out is widespread in tribal India. The practice of marrying outside one's clan is called EXOGAMY. A breach of exogamy brings disaster as the Khasi believe. It entails excommunication, refusal of funeral ceremonies and no resting place in the sepulchre of the clan.

Among some peoples the emphasis on marital partners tends to be "proscriptive" that is, the rules say whom a person shall not marry, and then leave freedom for selection outside this proscribed circle.

To marry within the forbidden degrees of kinship is to commit INCEST.

EXOGAMY is generally a characteristic of the clan system based on totemic designations. Exogamy is much more widely distributed than totemism.

Goldenweiser and many others have disputed a causal link between the two institutions.

Origin of Exogamy

Risely in his book on the people of India, says that probably there has existed in man a tendency to vary. This desire must have driven man to seek marital alliance with strangers, unfamiliar and unknown to him,

Westermark has recorded that when he asked one of the Berbers of Morocco why he did not marry within the village, he was asked in reply how he, the Berber, could do so, having seen all the girls growing up in the village along with him.

Such an aversion for familiar may be the explanation for the causes behind exogamy. This would, however, be in direct opposition to the neo-Freudian viewpoint viz. that sexual affinity between primary kin exists, and being in the nature of incest, such attraction must be repressed, and exogamy is one such social mechanism.

Malinowaski has pointed out the reality of incestuous feelings that do often manifest themselves in overt behaviour.

The very elaborate rules for the prevention of incest, which are universal, bear witness to such possibilities.

Audrey Richards,. on the basis of her researches among Africans, pointed out that psychologists and anthropologists have often overrated the role of sex, hunger being in reality a more fundamental and compulsive drive than sex. In hunting and food gathering societies, food is difficult to obtain. Women and children are generally a burden in such societies, particularly those which rely more on hunting. This could have led to female infanticide, which in consequence would lead to female scarcity. This must have led to marriage by capture, and as the next step—since such capture had to be effected from outside the tribe—to exogamy. Thus, food scarcity may be, historically speaking, a probable though not so plausible cause of exogamy.

Exogamy and Endogamy

The reverse practice of marrying within one's tribe, or very rarely, clan, is called exogamy. The two main clans of the Todas namely Tartharol and Teivaliol, are endogamous but their subdivisions, the Sibs, are exogamous. The Bhils also have two similar endogamous groups, the Ujabe Bhil and the Mele Bhil. Due to the universal fear of the strange, the novel and the unknown almost all Indian tribes are Endogamous. It is the fear of the neighbour's witchcraft and sorcery which is the prime cause for the Korwa Endogamy. Territorial, socio-cultural and linguistic units share enough thought and action patterns to want to preserve them by endogamy. Besides, territorial and linguistic factors impose limits on the communication of thoughts and persons (spouses) between various groups. However the barriers of endogamy have been broken down by several 'sophisticated' tribes like the Gonds, the Bhils and the Santhals, who have tried to get incorporated into the vast body of Hindu castes by marrying into the lower castes, the purpose of such a movement being the desire to rise in the estimation of the Hindu neighbours.

In contrast, many societies stress a 'prescriptive' principle. That is they indicate whom a person shall marry. The most widely known arrangement of this kind is known as CROSS-COUSIN—MARRIAGE. It implies a change or crossing over of sex, that is, a person's mother's brother's child or a father's sister's child. Such cousins are normally members of different households and may be from different communities.

In contrast, a person's father's brother's child or mother's sister's child is a PARALLEL COUSIN and in many cases would live close by or even with the same household. In a crosscousin marriage the preferred or required union for a man may be with his mother's brother's daughter or else with his father's sister's daughter. When the emphasis is on the side only, it forms an ASYMMETRICAL CROSS-COUSIN MARRIAGE. If the man can choose either cross-cousin, the marriage is called SYMMETRICAL. A particularly inwoven pattern is provided by a double cross-cousin marriage. Here a man marrying his mother's brother's daughter (*Mameri Bahin*) is at the same time marrying his father's sister's daughter. (*Phupheri Bahin*) A man's son marries the daughter of his sister, the latter being the wife of his own wife's brother.

Diagram

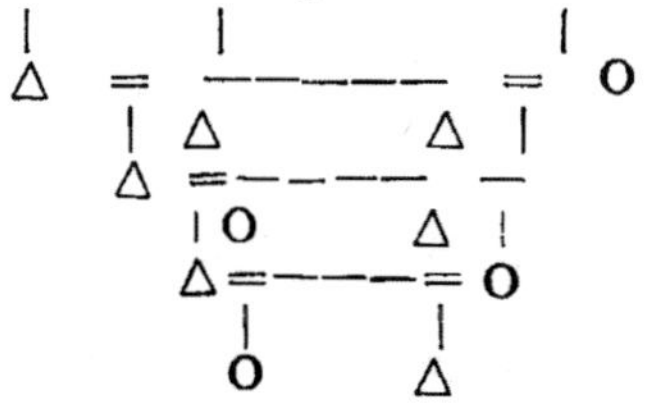

Two further examples of prescribed marriage may be cited. One is LEVIRATE, (*Devar Vivah*) familar through the old Testament, by which at a man's death his widow is expected to be taken over by his younger brother or equivalent kinsmen. It promotes inter familial cordiality by making certain linkages imperative. Among the TODAS the practice has been for one woman to marry several brothers (FRATERNAL OR ADELPHIC POLYANDRY).

In SORORATE a man may take or sometime has to take an additional wife or wives from among the younger sisters of his wife, either at her death or while she is still alive. It is generally found to prevail among tribes that pay a bride price for a wife.

POLYGAMY is a blanket term covering a great many

specific varieties of marriage system in which, with social approval, a person may have more than one marital partner.

Murdock reports 78 per cent polygamous families in his sample of 250. In tribal India also, polygamy is widespread.

Polygamy is of two types i.e. Λ =0,0,0

(i) POLYGYNY is the marriage of one man to several women. Naga, Gond, Baiga, Toda, Lushei etc are example of this type in Tribal India.

0=△,△,△

(ii) POLYANDRY shown in the above diagram is the marriage of one woman to several man. Tyan, Toda, Kota, Khasa, Ladakhi Botia, Nayarsam are preserving this type of marriage even totay.

Both types of marriage are referred to as polygamy in common parlance.

Khasi, Santhal, Kadar are MONOGAMOUS. Excessive high bride price has forced HO to be monogamous. Monogamy is that form of marriage in which one man marry with one woman.

Adelphic or Fraternal Polyandry

When several brothers share the same wife as among the Khasis and the Todas we have adelphic or fraternal polyandry.

Polyandry is not everywhere explicable with reference to a preponderance of men over women as was posited by Westermarck.

Group Marriage

If two or more husbands are married jointly to two or more wives it is group marriage.

Locality or Residence Principle

The locality or residence principle in marriage also lends itself for variation. The most typical procedures are for either the bride to go to live with, or in the same locality as, the husband's people, so-called PATRILOCAL (FATHER PLACE) residence or the husband to go to the brides locality, that is MATRILOCAL residence.

But the system may require, instead, residence first with the bride's family and later with that of the husband (MATRI-PATRILOCAL), alternating residence in both places (BIO-LOCAL OR AMBILOCAL) or residence at the home of the groom's maternal uncle that is one of his mother's brothers (AVUNCULOCAL). The married couple may also, as in the modern urban society set up a home apart from the parents of both : NEOLOCAL (NEW PLACE), where a local residential group normally marries in endogamous fashion so that all members are kinsemen. Murdock (1949) has called the result in community a DEME, after an old Attic Greek term. Kroeber (1938) has pointed to the importance of common residence as a basis of social action.

Hypergamy

Under the kind of social structure that caste has given rise to in India, there are certain restrictions in the form of limits beyond which a man and a woman cannot go in the choice of a spouse : of course, he or she must invariably marry outside his or her OWN GOTRA. Just as in modern times if a millionaire's daughter, who chooses to marry a pauper who will accept no doles from his father. in-law, would lose her economic status. Likewise, under the caste system, if a high caste woman marries a low caste man she loses caste status which is indicative of a degree of ritual purity. Up to marriage a daughter shares her father's caste status and after marriage her husband's. But a man himself does not loose caste status or ritual purity by marrying a low caste woman, though his offspring would suffer from a partial lowering from their father's caste status. Therefore, to prevent a woman from losing caste and becoming ritually impure, Manu and other ancient law givers prescribed HYPERGAMOUS (ANULOMA) marriage under which a man can marry from his own caste or from those below.

Men :

Brahmin—Brahmin, Kashatriya, Vaish, Sudra
Kashtriya—Kashtriya, Vaish, Sudra
Vaish—Vaish, Sudra
Sudra—Sudra

But a woman can marry only in her own caste or a higher HYPOGAMY (PRATILOMA). Marriage of a women to a man from a low caste is not permitted likewise for women.

Woman :

Sudra—Sudra, Vaish, Kashatriya, Brahmin
Vaish—Vaish, Kshatriya, Brahmin
Kshatriya—Kshatriya, Brahmin
Brahmin—Brahmin

For this system one has to pay high bride price. This has led to marriage by capture among the lower castes.

Ways of Acquiring Mates

1. Probationary Marriage—Kuki ete.
2. Marriage by capture—Naga, Ho, Kharia, Birhor. etc
3. Marriage by trial—Bhil etc.
4. Marriage by purchase—Naga, Rangwa, Ho etc. (Bride price).
5. Marriage by Service—Gond, Baiga etc.
6. Marriage by exchange—Khasi etc.
7. Marriage by mutual consent and elopement—Munda, Oraon, Maria, etc
8. Marriage by intrusion—Birhor, Ho etc

Inheritance of widows

Sema Nage one is often obliged to marry one's father's widow.

This is prevalent for inheriting property within family members.

Pre-marital and extra-marital sex relations

All over tribal India, pre-marital relations are generally free and much value is not set on virginity. Among the Konyak Naga a girl continues her amours even after her marriage. It is only when a child is born to her that she moves to her husband's household. It becoing known that the child is not his does not cause any inconvenience embarrassment.

In middle India, pre-marital liaisons are overlooked unless of course they lead to pregnancy which is generally regarded as shameful for the girl's parents, even if the pregnancy be caused by suitors or servant's attentions. The girl is asked to name the child's father and he is forced to marry her. No, or only reduced, bride price may be paid when such girls are married off.

Among some tribes, like the Muria, adolescent life is one of preparation for all the activities of adult life and in their dormitories grown-up girls are often found to train younger boys in the act of love and sex life.

Extra-marital relations

Extra-marital sex relations are not so easily tolerated. One of the main causes of Maria murder and suicide has been reported to be marital infedility. However, such sex jealousy is by no means universal. The Tharu men are so much under the thumbs of their beautiful wives that they take no offence at the latter's sex morals. The Khasi have developed a double standard of morality whereby a woman as a wife (Ranti) has to observe a strict sex morals code, but as a daughter (Dhyanti) has free scope to have as many liaisons and amours as she likes. In view of this, the Khasi women never completely cut off themselves from their parent's households. The strain which the Khasa wife suffers by being wife to several men, who are mentally and physically unlike each other, are relieved by the unfettered life of abandon which she can lead in her parent's village.

Divorce

Dissolution of marriage is difficult if it is regarded as a religious sacrament, which is not the case with Indian tribes. Consequently, we find that divorce is commonly practised, and may be obtained by either of the parties refusing to continue to live in wedlock, by abandoning the spouse.

The Khasi permit divorce for reasons of adultery, barrenness and incompatibility of temperament, but the separation can take place only after mutual consent. In some cases, the party desiring the dissolution may have to pay compensation to the other party. There is no possibility of remarriage between two such people as have separated by divorce. The divorce has to be a public ceremony. The mother gets the custody of the children. Among the Lushei, the dissolution of marriage is a much similar affair. If a husband turns out his wife, he must pay the balance of the bride price if any is due. However, if his wife deserts him or is caught in adultery, she has to arrange for the return of the bride price her husband paid for her. A second marriage between those once divorced is possible. Among the Kuki also, divorce is easily obtained.

The Gond allow divorce freely on grounds of marital infidelity, carelessness in household work, barrenness and quarrelsome disposition. Either party can take the initiative.

The Kharia also permit the right to demand dissolution to either party, on grounds of marital infidelity, sterility of the wife, laziness, refusal of the wife to live with her husband, theft and adjudication by the village Panchayat that the wife is a witch.

Widow remarriage has been practised all over tribal India, and the Hindu ban on such marriage has not as yet made any deep impact on tribal social organization, nor is it likely to do so in view of the popularization of widow marriage among *Hindus themselves.*

Children

Among the Tullishi, one of the Nuba hill tribes in Nilotic Sudan, as reported by Nadel (1947), it is the accepted rule that one pays for a girl as much as had previously been paid for her mother. The bride price called "wealth of marriage", is mostly calculated in cattle, though equivalents to the same amount may be given in other livestock, and occasionally grain or special tools and weapons including ceremonial spear points and hoe blades.

It remains with the women until her death and is divided among her children.

History of Human Marriage

The evolutionists, ever keen on building schemes of unilinear evolution, i.e. evolution in a straight line sought to establish a long chain of development at the lower end of which they put promiscuity, without any taboo even on incest, and at the top of which they put enforced monogamy as it prevailed in the 19th century Western Society. It may be pointed out that the startling conclusions regarding promiscuity and group marriage were drawn mostly from certain types of kinship terms which failed to differentiate between different kinds and forms of the laxity of sex morals in some preliterate societies. Thus among some of the tribes of Middle India, on festive occasions, some pre-marital and extra marital licence obtains, though the society is strictly monogamous, as is the case with elc Ho. In recent scientific formulations, based on moredata, the classification, rather than description, of kin as also the laxity of sex morals have been explained otherwise. Actually at the present moment, there is no evidence of promiscuity coming from simple cultures. In India, the simplest and the rudest of tribal cultures we know, e.g. The Andamanese, the Kadar, the Paliyan, the Malpantaram, the Chenchu, the Birhor and others, do not furnish us an evidence of promiscuity. In fact, monogamy and marital fidelity are reported from most of the tribes. Monogamy is the general rule, although it is not an obligatory one ; it obtains in the sense that there is a socially permitted marital relationship with only one person at a time.

Lowie sums up the position very well by stating that promiscuity, in the technical sense, must have undoubtedly existed at that point of history when the ancestor of modern man had not yet developed a culture with norms for judging sexual behaviour, but the very simplest of contemporary culture do not furnish any evidence of group marriage to enable us to substantiate the evolutionary scheme. Indian data as indicated above, are no exception to the rule. However, as Lowie points out, a state somewhat like that of group marriage is found as a recent development among the Toda, a tribe by no means one of the simplest in India. The Toda were formerly polyandrous and practised female infanticide. When the new system of law and order was introduced by the British, infanticide became a crime, and the sex ratio got more or less equalized. However the Toda did not give up polyandry as a consequence but developed polygyny also in association with polyandry. Thus whereas formerly several brothers married one woman, now they marry more than one woman. This nearest approach to group marriage, where no particular individual has exclusive marital rights over any of the spouses, is a recent development in a comparatively sophisticated society. A similar process of the emergence of group marriage has been reported from the Khasi.

In the light of above, the evolution of marriage as a sequential scheme is not acceptable. Westermarck takes the stand that marriage has in all probaility developed out of a primeval habit, and gets the support of Malinowaski, who believes that the family as a grouping has been taken over by man from the highly developed apes. However, it becomes difficult to accept the implication that monogamy is a natural instinct and a primeval habit in view of the fact that polygyny is very widely prevalent in the world.

From the data collected among Indian tribes, it is found that the restrictions, if any, on polygyny are more socio-economic than strongly moral or instinctive. Thus if every Ho does not live in a polygynous family, it is because he cannot afford to pay bride price over again.

To conclude, marriage and the family being two aspects of the same social reality, viz. the bio-psychical-cum-social drives (needs) of man, are coeval with each other and with culture, because without the marriage there could be no family.

A search into the origins of marriage is, therefore, unnecessary and not likely to lead us to any important and universal institution. Historical data are relevant only in finding out why a particular society has developed a particular form of marriage and not why the institution itself has developed.

3

FAMILY

Definition

Types

FAMILY

Definition

The family is a social unit, consisting minimally of a married couple and the children that couple may have. Families, as we define them, are as nearly universal as marriage. This is not surprising in view of the fact that nearly all societies have marriage, and immature offspring usually live with at least one parent.

The Dictionary of Sociology defines family as "the basic social institution. One or more men living with one or more women in a socially sanctioned and more or less enduring sex relationship, with socially recognised rights and obligations together with their offspring. Similarly in Encyclopaedia Britannica it has been defined as 'viewed abstractly, the most familiar of social institutions seems the most stable, enduring and universal. The family functions to satisfy certain universal needs which persist among all men in all times'. Maclver is of the opinion that 'The family is a group defined by a sex relationship precise and enduring to provide for the procreation and upbringing of the children'. Endorsing the view of MacIver, Burgess and Locke write that "The family is a group of persons united by the ties of marriage, blood or adoption, consisting a single household, interacting and intercommunicating with each other in their respective social role of husband and wife, father and mother, son and daughter, brother and sister and creating and maintaining a common culture'.

Thus family is the elementary unit of society consisting of parents and their children, own or adopted. It also includes a son-in-law in cases where a person chooses to have one at home (Ghar Jamaie) in the absence of a male issue. The members of a family (particularly the parents and their young children) usually share a common residence and acknowledge certain reciprocal rights and obligations, specially regarding economic activity. A person generally belongs in his life to at least one family—a family of orientation—the one he is born into. Later upon marrying, a person forms a new family—a family of procreation.

Family is the primary social institution. It satisfies the biological needs of its members particularly those of the expectant mothers and the infant child. It is the family in which a man seeks a secure satisfaction of his biological drives. It is a means of regular and channelized sex satisfaction with legitimate social sanction and social recognition. Family also transmits culture and tradition from one generation to another. It trains its members how to behave in different situations. It also imparts training in anticipating the behaviour. Further family educates its members in the field of their traditional occupation, mythology, religion, physical and social living, environment and so on and so forth. It is the family where one leaves how to behave with elders, siblings and youngers. Family also has socio-cultural functions. One learns language, art, dance, songs etc. in the family.

The family provides a learning environment for children. While no animal is able to care for itself at birth, man is exceptional in that he is still not able to do so many years afterwards. This is because, biologically, man matures late, he has few, if any, inborn or instinctive responses to simplify his adjustment to his surroundings, and he has to learn a repertoire of beliefs and values necessary for their own and their society's continuance. The basic functions of the family may be performed with varying degrees of effectiveness from culture to culture, and the details of the ways in which families within different culture systems carry out these functions produce remarkably differing results in the individual personalities of children and adults.

Types

The family is a universal institution. There is no civilized or savage society in the world in which we do not find a social institution like family. It can be classified into 'Nuclear' and 'Extended' on the basis of the population or size of the family. Nuclear family is that kind of family in which husband, wife and their unmarried children live together. Although the nuclear family occurs in all societies, it is the sole form of familial unit in only about one-fourth of them. In about half of the societies of the world the nuclear family is encrusted within some kind of extended family, a large kinship group that includes more than a single set of spouses and their children.

The second type of family, based on relationship, is consanguineous and conjugal family. Consanguineous family is that type of family in which the members living together are blood relative of each other. It is found among the Nayars of the Malabar hills. The conjugal family is based on conjugal relationship. The family of the Kharias of Chotanagpur is the best example of this type of family. The conjugal family is limited both in scope of membership and in duration. It can include no more persons than mated pair can produce within their time of fecundity. And it cannot endure for more than the life span of one and a fraction of generation. The fraction of a generation is that part of the life span after the marriage of the founding spouses, while the whole generation is the life span of the children that are born into it. Each conjugal family gradually wanes away as death takes its toll, until at last it is extinct. The conjugal family is a discontinuous social unit. Each is born and destined to die within the span of the century.

The other kind of family is known as family of origin or orientation. This is the family in which one is born. The next type of family is the family of procreation. This is the family one sets up after one's marriage.

The other category of family is based on the nature of marriage and number of spouses. In this category MONOGAMY is the more popular and prevalent. The independent conjugal family is possible only when marriage is monogamous, but monogamy as the sole permitted marital form exists in minority of human societies. One husband with one wife and their children live together in this kind of family. The family of Sauria Paharia, Munda etc. are the example of this kind of family.

Polygynous family are another classification of family based on the number of spouses. Within polygamous marriages we have drawn a distinction between polygyny and polyandry. Polygamy means multiple marriage ; polygyny means multiple women. Polygyny, therefore, is that form of family in which a husband has more than one wife at one time. Major tribes of the central India fall under this category. Bigamy is the more special form of polygamy in which the husband limits himself to two wives or a woman to two husbands. There are a number of social motives underlying polygyny as an institution. If a man has the means to support several wives, he is able to present a richer and better equipped household to the world. More women can prepare better clothes and food. If women's handicrafts are marketable or suitable for exchange, his household wealth will be enhanced. The polygyny works out best when a man's several wives are sisters. This is psychologically reasonable, in so far as sisters are more used to each other's way than unrelated women ; they are subject to the influence of emotional loyalty acquired in childhood as members of the same conj.gal family. As representatives of the same marriage group, their non-personal interests in the marriage are identical, which is not the case with unrelated women. Sororal polygyny is in effect an anticipation of sororate privileges.

In a polyandrous family a woman has more than one husband. The Todas of India fall within this category. The actual marriage of several women to one man is common. Usually the Toda polyandrous union is fraternal but not always so. A few polygynous marriages occur and quite a few monogamous ones. However, female infanticide results in a shortage of adult women, so brothers often band together as a group of husbands. Children are ordinarily betrothed in infancy and the boy gives progeny price payments two times a year all through his childhood. He also has to provide a buffalo to help pay funeral expenses of members of his betrothed family. Just before attaining puberty, the girl is deflorated by man from same clan other than her own. Then she is ready for marriage. Right after puberty, she is given a dowry and taken to the home of her husband. Although she may have been betrothed to just one man, it is understood that she is also the wife of all his brothers. Even a boy yet unborn may become her husband, along with his elder brothers, when he becomes of age. All the brothers live together and share their wife without friction and without jealousy. When the wife becomes pregnant, one of the brothers goes through a ritual of 'presenting the bow'. This makes him the sociological father of the ensuing child and the next couple of children to be born. There is no concern over whether he is biological father or not. After he has his share of offspring to sponsor, another brother presents the bow, thus making himself the father of the next group of children and so on. This disregard of biological paternity in favour of ceremoniously established sociological fatherhood is also manifest in a way reminiscent of Sakalava progeny price privileges. Occasionally, a Toda woman may leave her legitimate husband to live with another man without official approval, or she may take a cohabitant, who pays her husband for privilege; in either case, her subsequent children still belong to the man (her husband) who performed the bow and arrow ritual.

Polyandry in the Darjeeling district of West Bengal is restricted to the younger brothers of the man who performs the wedding rite with the wife. If the elder brother dies and the common wife has no children, she may break the polyandrous bond by first tying a string to a finger of her No. 1 husband's corpse and binding it to one of her own fingers. Then by severing the string, she symbolically destroys the marriage rite.

Family may further be classified in terms of residence. In American society, and in much of western Europe, a young couple usually establishes a place of residence apart from their parents or other relatives when they marry ; if they have not already moved away before that. Our society is so oriented toward this pattern of marital residence, NEOLOCAL (new place) RESIDENCE, that it seems to be the obvious and natural one to follow. Neorich in India, perhaps because they are financially able, begin earlier than usual to train their children to live away from home by sending them to boarding schools at thirteen or fourteen. In the army or at an out of town college, young adults learn to live away from home most of the year yet may return 'home' for vacations. In any case, when a young person is married, or otherwise established, he or she generally lives apart from his family.

Patrilocal : the son stays and the daughter leaves, so that the married couple lives with or near the husband's parents.

Matrilocal : the daughter stays and the son leaves, so that the married couple lives with or near the wife's parents.

Bilocal : either the son or the deughter leaves, so that the married couple live with or near either the husband's parents or the wife's parents.

Avunculocal ; both sons and daughters normally leave but the son and his wife settle with or near his mother's brothers.

Family may be further grouped into following categories on the basis of lineage.

Bilateral (two sided) : affiliates an individual more or less equally with his or her mother's and father's relatives of all types.

Patrilineal : (the most frequent rule) affiliates an individual with kinsmen of both sexes related to him or her through men only ; in each generation, then, children belong to the kin group of their father.

Ambilineal (or cognatic) : affiliates an individual with kinsmen related to him or her through men or women. In other words, some people in the society affiliate with a group of kinsmen through their fathers and others through their mothers ; consequently the descent groups show both female and male genealogical links.

Double descent family : affiliates an individual for some purposes with a group of patrilineal kinsmen ; thus two rules of descent, each traced through links of one sex only, are operative at the same time.

The last classification of the family is based on the surname ; patrinomic family : when this family surname is affiliated through father side it becomes patrinomic family. Munda, Oraon, Sauria Paharia etc. are its examples.

Matrinomic when the family surnames are affiliated through mother side it becomes matrinomic family. Ńagar, Khasi, Yanadi etc. are its example.

The another classification of the family is based on the size and population of the family. It is known as EXTENDED or JOINT family. Though we are accustomed to the family consisting of a married couple and their young children (called the NUCLEAR family), this is not the most typical family arrangement. The extended family is the most common form known to anthropology. It consists of two or more monogamous, polygynous or polyandrous families linked by a blood tie. Most commonly, a married couple and one or more of their married children live in the same house or household. The constituent nuclear families are linked through the parent child tie. However, an extended family is sometimes composed of families linked through a sibling tie ; this variant is called a 'joint family'. For example, such a family may consist of two married brothers, their wives and their children. Extended families may be quite large—containing many nuclear families and including three generations.

In a society composed of extended families, marriage does not bring as pronounced a change in life-style as it does in our nuclear family culture where the couple moves to a new residence and forms a new and basically independent family unit. In extended families, the newly weds are assimilated into an existing family unit. Extended families are most often found in agricultural societies. This is probably because the extended family allows for greater continuity of land ownership.

4

KINSHIP

Definition

Kinship usage

Kinship terms

KINSHIP

Definition

Kinship plays an important part in all human society, both in the regulation of behaviour between persons and in the formation of groups. Even in modern western society, where its range of operation is restricted somewhat the domestic family still survives. In the simpler societies a wide range of activities are regulated by kinship, and it is among them that kinship systems are seen in their most developed form.

The persons are kins when they are linked by socially recognized bonds of descent or marriage of both. Man is a unisexual animal, so that every infant has both a physical father and a physical mother. The young child may grow up in the care and protection of its physical parents, but in human society it may sometimes be reared by people who are not its physical parents, and it may take its place in society as the child of others. Everywhere a person derives his position in society in some measure from his parentage. He is expected to act in a specific way towards certain people because they are his kinsfolk. He is classed with them by outsiders whether he likes it or not. In most societies, the adult status of a child is comparatively little dependent on its physical ancestary or its rearing ; it is social parentage which determines where it may inherit, to what offices it may succeed, who are its kinsfolk and to what kingroups it belongs.

According to L.H. Morgan 'The study of kinship is the investigation of how social ties of descent and marriage are established, elaborated, fabricated, modified, forgotten or suppressed. how these ties are related to other manifestations of personal and social acting; how casual connection is distinguished from social kinship'.

A kinship system is usually taken to refer to the complex of rules in any one society (or section of a society) which, by governing descent, succession, inheritance, marriage, extra marital sexual relations, and residence, determines the status of individuals and groups in respect of their ties of consanguinity and marriage.

The people are kinsmen, when they share a common ancestor or one has descended from the other. The word 'ancestor' here means somebody standing in the social position of a father who had a child until the present generation is reached; or somebody standing in the social position of a mother, etc. An ancestor is not necessarily a forbear or progenitor in a biological sense, and the tracing of kinship links by genealogies (which are statements about social relationships) is a process different from that of the tracing of blood relationships by the genericist. The facts of procreation provide men-in-society with certain elements which they use for the expression of social relations. Different societies perceive the facts of procreation differently (in a sense the facts differ); but even if the facts are perceived in the same way they may be put to different social use. In their eagerness to dispel the wrong notion that the study of kinship is the study of blood relationships, anthropologists sometimes fall into the error of denying any connection between the two things. The procreation and rearing of children form a kernel around which a particular society evolves its own system of allocating rights and duties. Biology does not explain why any particular kinship system exists, but the engendering of children is the natural key to the elaborate social edifice known as kinship.

Kinship relations are sometimes called relations of consanguinity (q.v.) a term which, shorn of its biological implications, is a satisfactory way of showing that kinship is concerned with descent.

The relationships which flow through marriage are relationships of affinity (q.v.). And because kinship and affinity are closely linked the first term is often used to cover the second.

Some anthropologists regard the expression affinial kin as a solecism, it may well be, but it is impossible to speak of a kinship system without including marriage and its consequent relationships.

In many industrial societies the range over which kinship spreads, both in regard to functions and individuals covered, is (or is commonly thought to be) so narrow that the terms family (q.v.) and kinship tend to merge. But in fact the family is a crucially distinct arc of kinship. It is in the family that the society reproduces itself. The family supplies members to kinship and other groups. The basic elements in the family are ties of filiation (that is, the linkage between two adjacent generations), even though a particular form of the family (extended, joint etc.) may contain several generations.

The constitution of the family is a reflex of the wider kinship system. This system determines, by its rule of marriage, and descent, who may marry whom and the differences in the rights and duties which will accrue to children vis-a-vis their parents and their kinsfolk through these parents.

In formal analysis a primary distinction is made between unilineal and non-unilineal kinship.

The first is a kind of kinship in which the tracing of descent in one line (either through males exclusively or through female exclusively) to a common ancestor is an entitlement to membership of a discrete group (clan, lineage etc.). Such group is accordingly either patrilineal or matrilineal. In some societies both groups exist, so that an individual is at once a member of his father's patrilineal group and his mother's matrilineal group (double unilineal—sometimes called DUAL OR DOUBLE DESCENT system). Unilineal descent does not of course exhaust kinship ; in a patrilineally organized society a man must also have kinship relations through his mother. In a double unilineal system, while both parents are severally members of the same group as their child, he has kinsmen, (e.g. his father's sister's son or mother's son) who are not members of either of his unilineal groups. In societies lacking unilineal organization we may find what some anthropologists call DESCENT groups (bilateral descent groups and ramages). If an individual traces descent from an ancestor through any link and forms a group with other people descended from the same ancestor, he may be a member of several such groups ; and these groups taken together will have overlapping membership (Bilateral descent groups). If there are groups in which an individual may claim membership through different kinds of kinship tie, but he is at the same time forced to choose only one of these groups, we find a kind of distinct (non-overlapping) descent group which in certain respects resembles a unilineally constructed group (ramage). On the other hand, in some societies we find no descent principle at all. In such cases kinship is organized exclusively on the basis of a circle of relatives traced towards from an individual (kindred). A formalized kindred is definable in terms of the degree of cousinship to which it is traced. A kindred which is bounded by third cousins, for example, will include an individual's eight sets of great grand parents and their descendants. No two individuals, unless they are full siblings, can have exactly the same kindred. This kind of grouping is not a descent group because the members of it as a whole fail to share a common ancestor. My cousin on my mother's side, for example, does not have ancestory in common with my cousin on my father's side (unless certain marriages have occurred). Kindreds of this kind have a symmetry which springs from the reckoning of relationship by degrees of distance no account being taken of the sex of the individuals through whom a relationship is traced. Sex for sex, a relative on my mother's side is structurally equivalent to one occupying a similar position on my father's side. It is for this reason that such a system can be easily described in the language of English kinship—uncle, aunt, and cousin denote position which are balanced on either side of a given individual.

Because in a kindred an individual traces relationship through both parents, a kinship system which has no groupings other than the kindred is sometimes ealled bilateral or cognatic. But the terms are unfortunate because all kinship is bilateral (or cognatic) whatever the nature of the descent system. Moreover, formalized kindreds may be found in unilineally organized societies.

The terms multilineal and omnilineal are sometimes used for

systems of kinship which are not unilineal, but these words, by implying the existence of lines, suggest too much. There are no lines in a kinship system which knows no formal grouping other than the kindred.

Formal analysis is merely a first step in the understanding of kinship systems.

The qualities of any one system can be judged only in terms of, first, the extent to which kinship relationships and align ments occur, and second, the nature of the rights and duties by which particular kinship relations are defined. For example two societies may be classified formally as having patrilineal systems, but while in one of them patriliny may define the framework of groups on which the society as a whole rest (so that political, economic, and religious activities are closely interwoven with kinship, patriliny permeating society in toto), inl the other case patrilineal groups may be confined to loca organization, the wider institutions of society being based on non-kinship criteria. Certain parts of pre-communist China showed localized large scale patrilineages in a number of primitive societies, but the study of kinship in China cannot by itself take us very far in understanding the political, legal, economic, and religious framework of Chinese society as a whole.

Again, the rights and duties between an individual and a specific relative are not likely to be exactly the same even in systems which formally resemble one another closely. A man's relationship with his mother's brother in matrilineal society 'A' may well differ in some significant respect from the corresponding relationship in matrilineal society 'B'.

The nature of a particular kinship system can be comprehended only when what is implied in kinship is measured against what is implied in other modes of organization in the same society. The study of descent, rules of incest—and exogamy, kinship terminology, residence rules, rules of succession and inheritance and preferential and prescriptive marriage allow us to characterize a kinship system as an internally consistent unity ; we have then to move out of this system to gauge how far it is significant in placing people in their society, in shaping the relations between them, and in affecting their modes of activity (political, legal, economic and religious).

KINSHIP USAGES OR KINSHIP BEHAVIOUR

Avoidance

No behaviour pattern should be taken for granted as 'natural' even that between parents and children. As a matter of fact this particular pattern varies considerably in different cultures and in different social strata of the same culture. Though we may speak of behaviour patterns as social norms, it must not be supposed that an accepted pattern rules out the expression of individual sentiment, only that there is a customary mode of behaviour which is more or less generally accepted.

The behaviour between parents and children is frequently formally regulated when the latter reach the age of puberty, and even during infancy in kind of attention given by the respective parents is largely ruled by custom and varies from one culture to another. The pattern of behaviour observed between brother and sister varies greatly and is usually regulated by custom ; they may be easy companions, or may treat one another with ceremonial respect or even complete avoidance, or they may be close friends and economic partners yet present a rigid formality in each other's presence, on all subjects that are sexually toned. Behaviour between siblings of the same sex may be as between equals or may be regulated by seniority. The respect in which seniors are held may be shown in a traditional manner, but it is necessary to ascertain which relatives are regarded as seniors, as this does not necessarily tally with age, i.e. a man younger than ego may be classificatory father and hence a senior. The father's brother and the mother's brother may be treated quite differently, and this may have nothing to do with seniority but be dependent on the type of descent recognized. The mother's brother may be treated quite differently. With patrilineal descent he frequently exercises no control, but is treated with a degree of intimacy and affection which would not be shown to the father or his brother. With matrilineal descent the position may be reversed, the maternal uncle exercising authority; while affection is shown to the father and his brother. Again, where cross-cousin or parallel cousin marriage is customary, that uncle who is the father of the prospective bride or of the girl who theoretically should be regarded as such, may be treated in the manner properly adopted towards the father-in-law. The attitude towards grand parents may be one of respect due to age, though among many peoples persons two generations apart call one another companions and treat one another as such. The behaviour of persons of the opposite sex within family in a large kinship group is regulated by custom.

In many cultures some persons who stand in definite relationships to each other avoid one another formally. These persons are usually of the opposite sex and related by marriage e.g. the most common avoidance is between the mother-in-law and the son-in-law. Avoidance as a mode of behaviour is always said to express respect. The degree of avoidance may vary. Avoidance may be practised only between the persons actually related genealogically or by affinity who are addressed by a certain term, or it may be extended to all persons to whom the same term is used, however remotely connected. Tylor, explaining the avoidance kin relationship between son-in-law and mother-in-law, related casually to matrilocal residence. Later anthropologists questioned the validity of Tylor's conclusions since these were based on deceptive statistics. It is quite likely that such causal relation may in most cases be only a correlation.

Frazer and Frend based their explanations of the kinship usage of avoidance on the repugnance, among all societies for tabooed sexual relations. Frazer's explanation applies to such examples of avoidance as were reported from the very primitive Ceylonese tribe, the Vedda, viz. brother-sister avoidance, or limited social relations between brothers and sisters reported from the Trobriand Islands and, in fact, from all parts of the world. Should a brother in Trobriands happen to see his sister being wooed by man, or she making love to him, all the three will have to commit suicide. But among the Mundas, brother and sister may not live under the same roof nor even they may take food together. No kind of intimacy or familiarity can ever develop between them. Frazer assigns the purpose of avoidance as to prevent such sexual intimacy as would amount to incest.

Frend's psycho-analytical explanation, like Frazer's is based on sexual attraction and the need to prevent sexual intimacy between various kind of relatives. According to this explanation, a boy or a girl when young has an infantile sexual passion for the parent of the opposite sex. Training is, therefore, required to teach the child to overcome and repress this feeling. Family customs are the medium through which this training is imparted. The natural consequence is the rise of ambivalent emotions in the subject's mind who is sought to be pulled away from his/her parent, avoidance is observed to prevent any error on behalf of the subject in adult life in the observance of the norms of sexual conduct.

The above explanations of avoidance overestimates the sexual attractions. If the explanation is core of the human tendencies then why is it not a universal usage, and why should member of the same sex avoid each other. These explanations turn the primitive into a preoccupied conscientions thinker which he is not.

Lowie, explaining the avoidance syays that a daughter in law represents an alien and perhaps a different set of social, cultural and moral values. Her language, dress and notions about etiquette may be quite different from that of her husband's family. As an individual, her husband is bound to be influenced by her, but the rest of the family must not come under her influence. Hence the avoidance between her and her parents-in-law. Likewise, the son-in-law must be prevented from making cultural inroads into his wife's family.

According to Turney high avoidance is a mechanism to preserve peace in the family. A woman's loyalty as wife may come into conflict with her loyalties as daughter-in-law consequently, the authority of the parents-in-law might collide with that of the husband. This would subject the wife to severe strain and jeopardize the parents-son relationship. To prevent such social strains, daughter-in-law-parents-in-law avoidance is observed.

Radcliffe-Brown has given one of the most plausible of contemporary explanations. He points out that avoidance is a social fact and must, therefore, have social explanation. He says that whatever people come in contact with each other, the possibilities of cooperation as well as conflict are always equally present. But there are certain kinds of kinship where hostility is regarded as against social norms. The best way to prevent such hostility from becoming mainfest is to put restrictions on the development of intimacy ; and hence the kinship usage of avoidance.

In some societies to take the name of wife or husband is a considered taboo. To take the name of baby after evening is also a taboo. These taboos are out of affection.

Joking

The opposite pole to avoidance is extreme familarity, people who stand in certain relationship may commonly accost one another with buffoonery. This is commonly known as the Joking relationship. The relationship here again is not equal, one person stands as the butt of the other's wit, and though he can retaliate he must not take offence, and can only respond in a jocular manner. Free conversation on marriage or on sexual matters may be permitted between certain relatives. (Notes and queries in anthropology). The superficially free and easy relationship is sometimes called a joking relationship, since one or other (sometimes both) of the parties to it may take advantage of the other and abuse him jocularly without offence being taken. But sometimes, also, it involves certain formal restrictions and prohibitions, often of a ritual or symbolic kind (John Beattie, Other Cultures, 1964, p. 110).

Joking relationship may be indicative of equality and mutual reciprocity. They may also be indicative of potential sexual relationship. Thus is explained the joking relationship between a man and his wife's younger sister, or between a woman and her husband's younger brother. A joking relationship with one's maternal uncle's wife may be indicative of the practice of inheriting all the property of one's maternal uncle, includiug his wife. It may be indicative of a joking relationship with the maternal uncle himself, expressed through sexual intimacy with his wife. Such usages have been reported from the matrilineal Hopi and the matrilineal Trobriand Islanders.

Among many primitive folk joking relationships have been found to prevail between grand-parents and grand-children.

Such joking relationship is found among Oraon and Munda. S.C. Roy has reported an instance of a grand-father marrying his grand daughter among the Oraon. Verrier Elwin has reported a similar instance from the Baiga where a grandson married his own grand mother.

A joking relationship, when not mutual, assumes the role of social control. It becomes indicative of correction through ridicule.

In almost all societies the relationship between grand children and their grand parents is one of easy familiarity. Radcliffe Brown has summed this up in his phrase 'the merging of alternate generations'. He says that joking relations may be a kind of friendliness expressed by a show of hostility. Chapple and Coon regard this usage as the way to stimulate a higher interaction rate between various people which it may not be possible to do otherwise.

Kinship terms

Tenonym :

All over rural India, and among some tribal groups like the khasi as well and also elsewhere among the primitive societies of some parts of the world, a person is referred to as the father or the mother of his/her child i.e. taknonymously. Tylor regarded this kinship usage also as a relic of the former supremacy of women, who never accepted the son-in-law as one of them in their residence and recognized a secondary relationship with him through the children he helped to bring to life. Through extension, a mother may likewise be referred to tenonymously.

Avunculate :

If the maternal uncle enjoys a pre-eminent place in the life and affections of his nephews and nices as a matter of connection, if he has special obligations towards them which exceed those of their father, if he has a prior right over their loyalties, if he transmits his property to his nephew, and if the nephew works for him rather than for his own father ; in sum, if the maternal uncle comes first among all male relatives, then this kinship usage, is designated as AVUNCULATE, and the maternal uncle's authority as AVUNCUPOTESTALITY. If nephew and nices are brought up in their maternal uncle's family, the condition is referred to as AVUNCULOCAL residence. This is a common usage among patrilineal societies, as a result of diffusion (borrowing from outside) or as a survival of a previous mode of matrilineal social structure.

Amitate :

A special role, similar to that outlined in case of the maternal uncle, for one's father's sister is designated as AMITATE. Whereas amitate may be easily explicable in a patrilineal society, it has to be explained in the context of the matrilineal culture—complex of the Trobriand Islanders. It would seem that whereas avanculate in a matrilineal society and amitate in a patrilineal society may be the outcome of an obvious emphasis. On one particular group of relatives, such emphasis expressed through avunculate in patrilineal society and amitate in a matrilineal society may be the social mechanism for preventing certain kinship bonds from falling into neglect.

Couvade :

A queer practice designated couvade by anthropologists has been reported from among many primitive tribes like the Khasi and the Toda, as also from outside India. The practice consists in making a husband lead the life of an invalid along with his wife whenever she gives birth to a child. He refrains from active life, goes on sick diet and observes certain taboos. Thus the Khasi husband, like his wife cannot cross a stream or wash clothes until the spirits connected with childbirth are propitiated. This kinship usage involving wife and husband has been variously explained. Some authorities have found in it a survival of the transitional stage of the maternal-paternal complex. At the paternal stage there is no excuse for treating the father so, for patrilocal residence leaves no room for doubt concerning the paternity of the child. It is only at the maternal stage that paternity is not likely to be known nor is it considered important as the child takes the name of the mother's family and inheritance of property follows the uterine line of descent. In the maternal—paternal stage, where residence may be matrilocal, but inheritance patrilineal or conversely, some conventional methods of ascertaining paternity are needed keeping the father confined in a room or the customary bow and arrow ceremony of the Toda. The difficulty is that couvade is found associated with patriarchal clans and there is hardly any evidence to show that these clans at any time followed any system of inheritance other than the patrilineal. Malinowaski believed couvade to be a cementing bond of married life and a social mechanism designed to secure paternal affection. Raglan regarded it as an irrational belief which may be prior to marriage and even a contributory cause of the emergence of marriage as an institution.

Other anthropologists have sought to give a psychoanalytical explanation : they have attributed this usage to the husband's desire to lighten the wife's discomforts by a process of participation through identification. But of late other explanations also have been put forward. Thus it is said that a woman who has been delivered of a child undergoes certain chemical processes within her body which affect the atmosphere around her, if she is in an ill-ventilated cell or room making ill those other people who live and therefore breathe, in the same room. So it is said, couvade is based not on superstition but on a fact of course, illness would result only in a few cases and it has been, and is, only anticipated in all the remaining cases.

Thus anthropologists study kinship because in a great many small-scale societies all or most of the important kinds of institutionalized relatlonships between people are conceived in kinship terms. We cannot begin to understand these societies, and the ways in which their members order their affairs, unless we understand the kinship categories by means of which they do so. The study of kinship is centrally and essentially a study of other people's categories ; of the ways in which the members of other cultures think about kinship and about other people. Social anthropology is not and cannot be concerned with them also and essentially as involving systems of ideas and meanings. The study of kinship is not just a study of what people do ; it is also a study of what people think. For what they do is not fully intelligible until their modes of classification, their fundamental categories, are understood. Only then do their actual behaviour and its institutional implications make sense. Like much of social anthropology an important part of kinship studies consist of problems of translation.

Radcliffe—Brown has brought about much clarity of thinking in the field of kinship studies by his scientific treatment of the subject. He studies kinship systems with no preconceived notions regarding evolution as did Morgan. Rejecting any conjectural attempts at discovering origins, he studies kinship systems functionally and from the synchronic point of view, the aim being to understand the working of society at large at a time, or over time. Therefore, a marriage and kinship system is defined by him as being an arrangement which enables persons to live together and cooperate with one another in an orderly social life. And he regards the first step in the study of a kinship system to be the study of the kinship terms that are used.

Radcliffe—Brown has evolved certain generalizations which he designates as principles of kinship structure. Thus, there is his principle of inequality of proximate generations, the principle of the unit of siblings groups and so on. According to the latter principle, the solidarity of the sib-groups is expressed by the ego regarding all members of his own age group as siblings: he addresses them as such. Thus what is a diffused group becomes a well knit one. Exogamy as an unchangeable rule follows logically. Similarly the fact that the generation immediately senior to one's own is responsible for one's education and training,resulting in the need for the maintenance of its anthority, is expressed through the principle of inequality of proximate generations.

5

CLAN OR SIB

Definition

Functions

Difference between Family and Clan

Difference between Clan and Lineage

Clan and Community

Totemism

Moiety

Phratries

Double Descent

CLAN OR SIB

Definition

Clan is a fact of family. It acts as a second line of defence. Notes and Queries on Anthropology defines it as "A clan may be defined as a group of persons of both sexes, membership of which is determined by unilineal descent, actual or putative with *ipso facto* obligations of an exclusive kind". Similarly Glandys S. Richard defining clan mentions that "one sided inheritance of position as a member of either the male or female line is what constitutes the unilateral family, such family groups are designated as clans or genetes". Agreeing to it Jacob and Stern defines it as 'A unilateral pseudo-kinship relation pattern or group within a community. Clan members are such for life, practice clan exogamy, call fellow members sibligs if of the same generation, parents if of an older generation and son or daughter if of a younger generation.

A clan is an enlarged unilateral kinship group that rests on the fiction of common descent from a founding ancestor who lived so far in the distant past as to be mythological. Apart from size, the only essential difference between a lineage and a clan is that the members of a lineage can actually trace out their genealogies of common descent from known ancestor while clan members cannot. It they belong to a given clan, people believe they have common descent and their behaviour is regulated accordingly. Very often, however, the folklore of the clan includes a myth purporting to give a truthful account of how the clan came to be. The actual origin of the clan is lost in the hoary past, but this is not the case with lineages. Lineage may exist with or without clans, clans may also exist with or without institutionalised lineages within them.

Functions

The clan provides a large mutual aid organization on the footing of kinship. Man never stands alone. In seeking a firmer base for personal security than he can find without organization of his efforts and those of his fellow men, he casts about—for some valid interests of common concern that will serve to join him in social communion with others. There can be no doubt that the most generalized interest served by the clan is that of subserving the desire for security. The family is the incubator of personal security par excellence. The clan expands this fundamental function of the family by broadening the base in numbers of persons involved, while at the same time tightening up the structure by turning away from the diffusive effects inherent in extension along bilateral lines. To meet the needs of security, clan always present a solid front to the rest of the world. In their personal interrelations with all persons outside the clan, every clan member must be aided, abetted and protected at all hazards. From the implicit maxim that clan brothers should be helpful to each other, the principle of mutual aid and solidarity develops to the principle of collective procreation and its counterpart, collective liability. Motivated by the usage to provide personal security, clans move to punish wrongs and injuries suffered by any member as though all members were injured by the act. "Strike my clan brother and you strike me" is the challenge the tribal clansmen hurl at all comers. "The blood of the clan is my blood" is another precept of his code. The clan moves as a unit to wreak vengeance when murder has been done. The individual is strengthened in the secure knowledge that even though he may be wrong, his clan will stand by him. As a compliment of its united protection of individual members the clan is almost always collective liable for the acts of its member. Thus if a clansman commits murder, vengeance may commonly be taken on any member of the clan, for even though innocent in fact, his person is merged in that of his follow clansmen.

The security function of the clan inevitably leads it into the legal arena. In view of this, we may say that a second universal function of the clan is to operate as a legal instrument in the system of tribal law. Anthropoligists have recorded many instances in which a clan has cast out the blacksheep who is a continuous trouble maker. After all, clan solidarity cannot be a means of unbridled licence for irresponsible individuals. For the incorrigible rascal, clan disowner is tantamount to the death sentence in many societies for then the outcast may be assaulted with impunity. There is no protection for him outside the clan. Extension from the clan may come not only from having caused the clan too much trouble vis-a-vis clans, but also from persistent refusal to carry out one's coöperative obligations within the clan.

Another universal fuction of the clan is to regulate marriage by means of exogamy. This if we follow Malinowaski's bypothesis, it is a self protective device to ensure clan solidarity by directing the sexual drive toward persons outside the essential kinship group. We would do wrong, however, to overlook the fact that an additional security device is to be found in clan exogamy. Marriage imposes affinial obligations on the spouse's clan. It tends to reduce overt aggression between the the maritally allied groups ; it also extends the base of support a man may count on.

Another function that the clan may taken is that of government. Many tribes have raised one clan to the position of royalty, and the hereditary chief must come from this clan.

Among clan organised tribes practicing shifting cultivation the cultivable land is almost inevitably owned or administered by the clans. Clan may own other material goods in common, such as temples, meeting houses and sacred and ceremonial objects.

Difference between Family and Clan

1. Family is bilateral group whereas clan is unilateral group. Kadar tribe are bilateral. No example of unilateral family.
2. Family may extinct but clan never extincts ; clan is a continuous process.

Family breaks with the death or divorce of the either husband or wife but clan never breaks.

3. Family is universal but clan is not. Tribe like Kadar, Shampen, Onge etc. do not have clan.
4. Members of the family are close relatives but the members of the clan are close as well as distant relatives.

Difference between Clan and Lineage

1. Lineage is the larger social group and clan is its part i.e. patrilocal or matrilocal denotes the man/women from whom it originated and clan acts as thread in organising and grouping them in clans.
2. Lineage consists of the members of 3 to 11 generations, whereas clan consists of the members of unlimited generations.

Clan and Community

Clan is a smaller part of the community. There may be various clans in one community.

Totemism

Totemism is to trace the origin of lineage with any natural object life or lifeless e.g., stone, tree, animal, star, planet, sun, river, mountain, bird etc and to identify themselves as their descendants and to worship such imaginary or real object is totemism.

In Notes and Queries on Anthropology it has been defined as "the term totemism is used for a form of social organisation and magico-religious practices of which the central feature is the association of certain groups (clan or lineages) within a tribe with certain classes of animate or inanimate thing". Endorsing the basic feature of totemism Jacob and Stern mention that 'A serviceable though narrow definition would confine totems or totemism to certain phenomena of those special areas where there are clans each of which has an animal or bird name, and where the clan members believe themselves descended from their own clan animal or bird ancestor refuse to eat its flesh or wear its fur, and also conduct magical rites of one or another kind that relate to such a creature'.

Herskovits is of the opinion that 'Totemism is the belief that a mystical relationship exists between a group of human beings who make up a kinship unit and a species of plant or animal or less commonly some natural phenomenon'.

Similarly Golden-weiser defines tolemism as 'when we refer to totemism we mean that a tribe has a social organization, usually of the sib pattern, which is associated with a form of supernaturalism, consisting of certain typical attitudes toward species of animal or plants or classes of natural objects.

Theories of Origin of Totemism

Anthropologists were much confused about totemism till Goldenweiser wrote his celebrated essay on the subject in 1910. Till then attempts had been made by Lang, Durkheim, Frazer, Rivers and other to explain it. Some of them tried to show this association as nothing mystical or meaningful only a typical procedure of assigning names. Hopkins pointed out that cattle supplying food, as is the case with the Toda buffaloes, may be looked upon with reverence. Durkheim saw in totemism the emblem of the collection representation of the social mind. Tylor said that the primitive belief that after a person's death, his soul takes abode in certain animal or plant species and so the entire species is protected. Boas and Swanton think that totemism is an extension of the personal relation of an individual with an animal or plant. Goldenweiser points out that no omnibus solution to this riddle of totemism could be useful because the complex of totemism varies and differs from place to place and all its so-called typical features are not to be found everywhere. He regarded it as socio-religious institution. Risley said that in India the religious aspect of totemism is dead and only the social aspect is operative.

Elwin has reported that totemism may be the outcome of a historical accident or intimation i.e. diffusion. S.C. Roy regards that Fusion—coming together of several people and adopting one common name, Fission—splitting into smaller groups, Generalisation—would explain the emergence of totemism. In the light of the popularly believed stories about the emergence of clans among the Ho, it has been shown that in most cases it was an accidental relation between the individual and a plant or animal which was later on generalized.

Moiety

Reciprocity is the basis of all social relationships, for there can be no social relations without interaction. Human beings are so constituted that the isolated person is not a complete man. They are also so constituted that dependence without interdependence is not readily or for long accepted by the giver of services. He who gives would also receive. Through the building of a network of giving and receiving of services a society expands its potentialities.

The principle of reciprocity is, therefore, operative in all societies. However, some societies are content to leave it implict in their cultures without placing much formal emphasis upon it. One of the most effective ways of institutionalising reciprocity is to organize the society on a moiety basis. This is done by dividing the society in two equal halves or moieties, to produce a system known as dual division. Moieties are exogamous with few exceptions, each moiety supplies the other with its marriage partners. Other reciprocal services are invariably linked to the Moiety alignments. Moieties thus effectively control certain types of behaviour and serve to give concrete form to the reciprocity principle. In cases where there are only two clans in a tribe, clan and moiety are automatically synonymous. Multiple clans are the more common order, however, and when clans are linked to moieties, the moiety is the larger unit and the clans are sudivisions of the moieties. Although Morgan assumed that moieties precede clans in historical development, Lowie has rightly concluded that either one may precede the other, dependent on circumstances.

Phratries

Phratries are groups of linked clans, where there are more than two such linked groups in tribe. The clans in a phratry system retain their separate identities but each clan in a phratry feels some sort of special identity to the others within its phratry. Moreover, they may have special obligations to fulfil toward each other. Nevertheless, it may be said in general that phratry organization is a relatively rare and functionally insignificant phenomenon. It does not usually control marriage. For the most part, the phratry sentiment seems to rest either on a tradition of common origin or common interest in ceremonial activity.

Double Descent

It is also called bilineal descent. Anthropologists generally consider that a society could embrace only one clan system, which had to be either matrilineal or patrilineal. Evidence to the contrary first caught to the attention of R.S. Rattry's studies of the Ashanti, who were shown of African tribes to have matrilineal clans called ABUSUA and patrilineal groups called NTORO. The ntoro principle of inheritance is associated with the semen, and although the ntoro group is not organized, it regulates marriage and sets certain incest prohibitions. It is totemic and imposes certain food taboos on its members. Herskovits has indicated that double descent is probably quite widespread in West Africa. Australian class system of marriage combine matrilineal moieties, which are unnamed, with patrilineal clans. Murdock has thrown the phenomenon into focus by showing that double descent has wide distribution in India. That it took English speaking anthropologists so long to discover double descent shows how difficult it is for even carefully trained scientists to formulate conceptions necessary to the perception of new facts when those facts are too alien to their experience and cultural background.

6

RELIGION

Definition

Profane–Sacred

Distinction between :

- Religion and Magic
- Science and Magic

Animism

Anamatism

Manaism

Religion in Tribal India

Taboo

Totem

RELIGION

Definition

Religion is the human response to the apprehension of something or power which is supernatural and supersensory. It is the expression of the manner and type of adjustment effected by a people with their conception of the supernatural.

Religion had been regarded as a product of civilization until Tylor gave convincing proof that primitive societies have their own versions of religious activity, not very different from that of civilized societies.

Etymologically religion is derived from the Latin Word religio which is derived from either the root Leg-which means to gether count or observe, or from the root Lig-which means to find. In former sense the implication is belief in, and observation of, signs of Divine Communication. In the latter sense the implication is the performance of necessary actions which may bind together man and the supernatural powers that be. Both the implications are relevant in view of the fact that beliefs and rituals have been found to be the main component parts of religions everywhere.

All religions consist of a mental attitude regarding the supernatural. The most widespread manifestation of this attitude is the shape of beliefs and rituals. All religions, primitive and modern have this base of belief and ritual.

What differentiates the so-called higher religions from the primitive variety is the relative absence of philosophical speculation in the latter. Primitive man has not been found to be given to philosophising as much as the modern man. However, presence of religion of one kind or another has been always reported and today it is an essential feature of human life without which attainment of full integration of the human personality is not possible. Occupation of the exact nature of the supernatural differs from society to society, people to people. For religion, as an aspect of supernaturalism, consist of systems of belief, thought and action that lie at the veryroot of all primitive and civilized cultures. These systems of belief and action work upward and outward throughout the cultural fabric. At points they are woven so finely into the total pattern that it is impossible to say where the religion ends and the mundane begins. Religion presents so many aspects, intertwined with so many phases of culture, and is so variable that it is difficult to delineate it in terms both broad enough to encompass the whole and discriminating enough to isolate it for study.

The crux of the problem, is, then, first to examine the nature of what is meant by supernaturalism. It clearly implies a dichotomy of ideas : that which is natural and that which is more than natural, indeed, superior to the natural. In any thought system the difference between the two depends upon a people's general philosophy as to the nature of things, on their basic existential postulates and the way these are worked out in their world view. What is seen as natural and what is supernatural is relative to the culture of the moment. In our own system of knowledge many things that we once viewed as supernatural have now been moved over into the area of the natural. It is often said that religion exists in the areas of things that man cannot understand, that religion provides answers to the unanswerable. It is also said, in a like vein, that religion is based on fear. Both these assertions are true in part, but only in part. All cultures consist of solutions to problems. As religion is an aspect of culture, it also shares the quality of set solutions to problems. Religion, like culture, produces understanding in terms of the assumptions it makes. The essential difference between the natural and the supernatural lies in the qualitative emotional (affective) attitudes of mind and feeling.

Profane-Sacred

A classification of what is meant can be more readily achieved when put in the term advanced by the French sociologist Emile Durkheim who contrasted two polar attitudes: that which looks upon certain things as profane, and others as sacred

Profane	*Sacred*
The sphere of the routine, mundane taken for granted, work-a-day world.	The sphere of unusual extraordinary, not to be taken casually "out of this world".
Attitude : blase acceptance on a basis of common familarity.	Attitudes : awe, sense of mystery, circumspection in dealing with something special.

The term profane and sacred, so used, have meanings somewhat broader than ordinarily accorded them in common English usage. The profane is that which is taken naturally, the sacred supernaturally. The natural works in ways that are accepted as ordinary, as in accord with daily experience. The supernatural works in ways that are looked upon as unusual and special. The emotional connotations are consequently different. They are the product of human mental states. Magic and Religion rest upon a belief in the supernatural and they are basically matters of ideology and the kinds of feeling that accompany them.

Defining Magic Frazer mentions "Magic is an inventory of beliefs and forms of behaviour which are not subject to criticism, recheck and elimination". According to Malinowaski 'Magic is the wishful thinking over hopeful behaviour. Magical processes are utilized when people cannot proceed with other material techinques. Though magic, deities and supernatural powers are controlled, while through religion, they are pleased by presenting sacrifice to them, as well as by offering prayer'.

Distinction between Religion and Magic :

Religion	*Magic*
1. It is a social act.	1. It is an individual's act.

2. It is for the welfare of the world.	2. It is for the welfare of an individual.
3. Results of prayer may or may not be successful.	3. Prayer offered for achieving the aim.
4. Man surrenders to superpower.	4. Man controls the unknown power.
5. Religion comes after magic.	5. Magic comes before religion.
6. Mantras are recited correctly and God understands the feelings of the devotee.	6. Wrong recitation of Mantras minimises the power of Mantras.

Distinction between Science and Magic :

Science	*Magic*
1. It is real and true.	1. It is not true and is artificial.
2. If one failed in achieving the target one may try again until the desired results are not	2. If one failed, it lowers the prestige of magician and there is no question of further trial for achieving the goal.
3. Science is based on physical phenomenon	3. Magic is a mental phenomenon.
4. Science is based on worldly laws.	4. Magic is based on Ghost and evil spirits.
5. Science is experimented in laboratory and we are sure of its result.	5. No experiment in magic. We believe in the power of magic and are not sure of its results.

Animism

What are the forms that the supernatural ideas take place. Basically, they may be broken down into Animism and Mana. Animism as defined by E.B. Tylor, is the belief in spirit beings. We all know them by name viz. souls, ghosts, goblins, poltergeists genil, trolls, sprites, elves, pixies. leprechans, fairies, witches, demons, devils, angels and gods. Their essential quality is their ethereal embodiment, they are beings without real flesh and blood, non-material, but real enough for those who believe in them.

As spirits they are not subject to the laws of nature. They are uninhibited by the limitations of physical matter, by the weaknesses of human flesh. They transcend matter, time and space. They are supernatural. It is this that makes them wonderful mysteries. Tylor examined many manifestations of animism among primitive but his interests were more than just to describe its forms. Tylor saw the origin of animism in the phenomena of dreams of life and death. Dreams are a form of hallucination, an illusory experience.

Thus animism is the earliest anthrolopogical theory about primitive relgion, seeking to trace its origins and explan it, was given by Tylor, He said that although the origin appears to be multiple yet there is only one idea underlying it viz., belief in the Soul (ANIMA) hence the name animism for this theory.

Anamatism

Everything has life and is animate. Tylor's earliest critics said that animism is a later development in the history of religion. They postulated a pre-animistic stage when religious belief supposedly consisted mainly in the belief that everything has life and is animate. Prominent among these writers were Preuss and Max Muller.

Manaism

Supernaturalism finds its expression not only in beliefs in spirit beings ; there are also beliefs in the existence of supernatural forces that do not emanate from any kind of being. Such forces are expressed as special attributes of things much in the way that the force of gravity is related to objects that have mass. More recently, R.R. Marett evolved a special form of animalist theory which he called Manaism.

Mana is a force but not a vitalistic force. It exists as a supernatural attribute of persons and things. Above all, it is the exceptional power to do things that are unusual. Mana, therefore, manifests in the unusual, when the unusual is not the work of spirits. The entire religious life of the primitive is born out of their belief in a certain understandable, nonmaterial and unindividualized supernatural power which takes abode in all the objects, animate or inanimate that exist in the world. It lies more or less beyond the reach of the senses but is manifested as physical force or such other excellences as man can think of in himself, others and also in objects around him. It may differ in intensity, the degree in which it is present in a personal object but essence is always the same. The power that is extraordinary is not mundane force. It does not follow the regular laws of ordinary technologies or skills. Like the power of spirits, it transcends the natural. Mana is supernatural. Bonga among Ho tribe of Chotanagpur is its example.

The Manaism has been further critised like the earlier theory of Tylor. It invests the primitive with an aptitude for thinking. and rationalization which he does not actually possess.

Max Muller is of the opinion that earliest form of religion must have been the worship of objects of nature. The archaeological excavations conducted in Egypt and elsewhere support it. However, the critics say that reverence towards objects of nature is born as a result of a 'diseased' mind which invests lifeless things with life and all the power that is associated with life. This error of mind is born out of defective language. Such linguistic errors as the sun rises, sun sets, thunder, storms rain, trees or flowers and fruits give rise to belief in some power inherent in the sun, thunder, trees etc. Any claim to such worshipping the earliest form of religion is not convincing. The merit and usefulness of these various theories emerge when they are taken together as each of them expresses some essential truth regarding primitive religion.

Malinowaski points out with referenceto the Trobriand Islanders that religion is intimately connected with various emotional states, which are states of tension i.e. their magical and religious practices centre round the fishing expeditions. These are the outcome of the state of fear which a possible disaster on the seas gives rise to, similarly, hate, greed, anger, love etc. may arise due to various situations in a man's life. Religion has the function of bringing about readjustment between man and the supernatural in upset states of existence. It is a device to secure mental and physical stability in an individual's life.

Radcliffe-Brown takes a different stand. The function of religion is not to purge fear and other emotional strains from the human mind, but to instil a sense of dependence on society and thereby obtain the individual's concurrence with the social norms, the ultimate aim being social survival.

Religion in Tribal India

Tribal India presents a colour panorama of religious faiths and practices which is the manifestation of adjustments with their cultural ecological conditions. In tribal India the entire socio-econo-politic life moves around religion. Life, world view, ethos and ecology of the Sauria Paharia tribe of Bihar is not interwoven with the religion that one cannot understand them without understanding their religion. Their Hossaiyans and Addas are so dominant that they cannot ignore them even at the smallest moment of their life. Among the Korwas there is a spirit presiding over crops – one over rainfall, one over cattle. Besides there are several spirits which dictate the attitude of the Korwas towards their neighbours, priests, headmen etc. We will seldom get a tribe in India which do not believe in conversion of soul of the deceased into a potential spiritual force. Ancestor worship is widely prevelent among them. The Todas of Nilgiri Hills and the Hos of Chotanagpur perform two kinds of ceremonies after cremation. The second one is meant to make it sure that the departure of the soul from the body is final and forever. The Todas while returning from such ceremony, scatter thorns so that the malevolent soul may not enter their village. Majority of the tribals believe that life does not ends with death and that it continues to be present in one form or the other. The tribals of Chhattisgarh involve the spirits of their ancestors through special ceremonies. It is further believed that certain objects are possessed by some spiritual powers and thus a short of fetishism appears to be the guiding principle among such tribes.

In tribal India we find Hinduism as a widely prevalent religion. However, a good number of them have embraced christianity under the influence of various missionaries. These missionaries are well known for their role of the agent for religious. social, economic and educational change in tribal India.

Taboo

Taboo is an inevitable element in supernaturalism. Supernatural power is implicitly dangerous. We have referred to taboo as negative magic. It is used to designate all the restrictions, communicated through verbal 'Don't, Do's and generally associated with ritualistic behaviour, which a member of a primitive society has to submit to. In content taboo consists of a series of negative rules, each of which states a form of behaviour that will cause a supernatural power to backfire and injure the use. In reality, very few tabooed acts are physically or socially dangerous. The fuction of a taboo is predominantly psychological, originating in man's fear of dealing with forces he does not wholly understand. It also engenders respect and cautions care for the supernatural. In as much as supernatural power always involves taboo, no man can ever take his possession of power wholly for granted. Violation of a taboo not only nullifies the positive power of medicine, it may bring disaster as a consequence. Taboo is also an essential ingredient of social morality. It applies not only to the requirements of care in handling supernatural objects ; it can and is applied to social standards of behaviour that are not directly associated with the supernatural but in which it is held that the supernatural takes an interest. Incest is commonly subject to supernatural punishment, as well as to social sanctions, in most societies. Taboo, therefore, functions to sustain the awesomeness of the supernatural by reinforcing attitudes of care and mystery and by punishing attitude of carelessness and profanity in dealing with the supernatural. It also sustains the social system by using supernatural sanctions to punish social deviants and would be heretics. Radcliffe-Brown considers taboo as a social mechanism by which an orderly society is able to maintain itself in existence.

Totem

The sibs bear the name of animals and plants, other natural phenomena also. This mode of designation is fairly often coupled with beliefs and practices. The totem object is held sacred and there is strong sense of kinship with it on the part of the sib. Some time sib groups are not named after plants or animals but are nevertheless definitely associated with them, say, through the performance of rites for the magical multiplication of the correlated fauna or flora. The sib group believe themselves to be the descendant of the totem. All these and similar usages are brought together under the head of Totemism and the animal plant or object in question is called TOTEM.

Totem is found everywhere like Kerketta, Kacchap, Sandilya etc. Being world phenomenon the anthropologists assumed without further enquiry that all the phenomena—labelled totemism represented identical psychological processes and had originated independently in different areas through psychic unity of mankind.

Prof. Eliotsmith broaching the hypothesis that totemism developed in or about North-Eastern Africa and then spread to the four corners of the globe.

It was in 1910 that Dr. Goldenweiser approached totemism from a quite distinct point of view. Prof. Boas had reportedly shown that apparently simple ethnological phenomena were as a matter of fact the result not of primary unity but of secondary association. Further Boas had proved that the resemblance noted between remote tribes were often illusory ; they represented no basic likeness comparable to the homologies of the anatomist but rather correspond to his superficial analogies. That is to say, ethnologist had erred in the same sense in which the untouched mind errs when it classifies the whale as a fish and the bat as a bird. Applying these principles to what had been regarded as a uniform complex of features Goldenweiser discovered that totemism, instead in being everywhere alike, differed to an extraordinary degree.

7

POLITICAL ANTHROPOLOGY

Difinition

Significance

Devel opment

POLITICAL ANTHROPOLOGY

Definition

Political anthropology is a late specialization of social anthropology, whose theories, methods and results it attempts to present in a critical fashion. It proposes an initial synthesis and a general consideration of those political societies—alien to Western history—revealed by the anthropologist. These different aims involve, of course, certain risks—risks that are accepted in so far as all scientific knowledge is vulnerable and partially open to question. An undertaking of this kind could not have been envisaged without the progress already attained, during the past forty years, by means of direct research, which has extended our knowledge of 'exotic' political systems, and of the most recent theoretical research. The African anthropologists and sociologists have made an important contribution to this task, which explains the way references to their work.

Political anthropology appears both as a project—a very old, but ever present one—and as a late specialization of anthropological research. In its first aspect it is an attempt to transcend particular political experiences and doctrines. It tends therefore to the establishment of science of politics, regarding man as Homopoliticus and seking properties common to all political organizations in all their historical and geographical diversity. In this sense it is already present in Aristotle's 'Politics', which considers the human being as a naturally political being and attempts to discover laws, rather than lay down the best conceivable constitution for any possible state. In its second aspect, political anthropology is a subdivision of social anthropology or ethnology. It is concerned with the description and analysis of the political systems (structures, processes and representations) proper to societies regarded as primitive or archaic. In this sense, its existence as an independent discipline is of recent date. R. Lowie has contributed to its construction while deploring the inadequacy of anthropological work in the political field.

In the last three decades this tendency has been reversed. Field work has increased, particularly in Black Africa, where over a hundred 'cases' have been observed and can be subjected to scientific treatment. Theoretical developments are beginning to emerge from the results acquired through this new research. This sudden progress may be explained as much by present day events—the consideration of ex-colonial societies now in the process of transformation—as by the internal development of anthropological science. Political scientist now recognise the necessity of a political anthropology. G. Almond sees it as the pre-requisite of any comparative political science. Raymond Aron states that the 'underdeveloped' societies are likely to fascinate political scientists who wish to escape from Western or industrial provincialism (1965) and C.N. Parkinson remarks that 'some could conclude that the whole subject (the study of political theories) were better taken from the historian and handed to the social anthropologist (1958).

Significance

As a discipline aspiring to the status of a science, political anthropology is first of all a mode of recognition and knowledge of 'other', exotic political forms. It is an instrument for the discovery and study of the various institutions and practices that constitute the government of men, and the systems of thought and the symbols on which they are based. When Montesquieu develops the notion of oriental despotism (suggesting an ideal type in Max Weber's sense), places the societies thus defined in a class of their own and reveals political traditions different from those of Europe, he shows himself to be one of the earliest founders of political anthropology. Indeed, the place accorded to this model of political society in

Marxist and Neo-Marxist thought is proof of the importance of this contribution.

Montesquieu is, in fact, the initiator of a scientific enterprise that for a time performed the role of cultural and social anthropology. He draws up an inventory showing the diversity of human societies, based on ancient history, travellers' descriptions and observations concerning foreign or strange countries. He sketches a method of comparison and classification, a typology ; this lead him to give particular value to the political sphere and, in a way, identifies the types of society according to their modes of government. With a similar aim in view, anthropology first attempted to determine cultural areas and sequences on the basis of technico-economic criterion, the elements of civilization and the forms of the political structures. (T.H. Steward remarks in this connexion : The socio-political structure lends itself to classification and is more readily formulated than are other aspects of culture-1966) Thus the 'political' becomes a relevant criterion for the differentiation of whole societies and civilizations : sometimes it is given a privileged scientifie status. Political anthropology is seen as a discipline concerned with 'archaic' societiees in which the state is not clearly constituted and societies in which the state exists and takes on a wide variety of forms. It must of course confront the problem of the state's origins and earliest forms : in devoting one of his principal works—"The Origin of the State" (1927) to this question, Lowie returned to the same pre-occupations as those of the pioneers of anthropological research. It is also confronted by the problem of segmentry societies, without a centralized political power, which are the object of an old, but ever present debate. The historian F.J. Teggart, who is often quoted by the British anthropologists states : 'Political Organization is an exceptional thing, characteristic only of certain groups—all people whosoever have once been or still are organized on a different basis' (1918). Thirty years later, the American anthropologist R. Maclver continues to admit that 'tribal government differs from all other political forms' (1947-158) either by essential difference or by the absence of the political, the socicties relevant to anthropological study are in a class of their own. Simplistic dichotomies are proposed to explain this position. Societies without political organization/ societies with political organization, without a state/with a state, with a history or with a repetitive history/with a cumulative history etc. These oppositions are very misleading, they create a false epistemological distinction through the old distinction between primitive and civilized societies had a decisive influence at its inception. Postponing the methodical study of 'primitive systems of political organization', anthropologists have opened the way to negative interpretations by theoreticians, foreign to their discipline, who deny the existence of such systems.

The transformations that are taking place in the developing societies give an additional significance to the co-operative efforts of political anthropology. They make possible the contemporary and non-retrospective study of the processes that govern the transition from tribal government and the traditional state to the modern state, from myth to political doctrine and ideology. It is a time particularly suited to such a study, one of those periods of profound change such as Saint Simon envisioned in the industrial revolution, a period that sees the formation of a new type of society and civilization. The present situation of the 'exotic' political societies encourages one to examine, with due regard to the dynamic nature of the situation, the relation between traditional and modern political organizations, between tradition and modernism ; moreover, in subjecting the first to real test, it requires a new, more critical view of them. The confrontation goes beyond a study of the diversity and origin of political forms ; it also poses the problem of their inter-relations in general, of their incompabilities and antagonisms, their adaptations and their mutations.

Development

Although political anthropology is primarily the consideration of political exoticism and the comparative analysis that results from it, its origins are very ancient indeed. Political phenomena were considered by the early anthropologists above all from the point of view of origin and with such obvious hesitation that one may well conclude that they had no real interest in the field. Gluckman denounces the complete inadequacy of their contribution to it. No early anthropologist, not even Maine, if we can claim him as an ancestor, had dealt with political problems, perhaps because all the earler researches in anthropology were done on the small scale societies of America, Australia, Oceania and India and its Islands (1963). However, there are frequent references to the pioneers. For example, Sir Henry Maine, who was mentioned above and who is often neglected. His famous work ANCIENT LAW (1861), a comparative study of Indo-European institutions, reveals the existence of two 'revolutions' in the development of societies based on contract ; the change from social organizations centred on kinship to organizations governed by another principle notably that of "Local contiguity", which defines 'the basis of common political action'. This double distinction lies at the origin of a debate that is still alive today. But the most frequently quoted reference is still ANCIENT SOCIETY (1877) by L.H. Morgan, the inspirer of Engels and the revered father of most modern anthropologists. He recognizes two 'fundamentally distinct' kinds of government significant for the early development of societies. The first is the order of time, is founded upon persons, and upon relations purely personal, and may be distinguished as society (SOCIETAS) . The second is founded upon territory and upon property, and may be distinguished as a state (CIVITAS)—political society is organised upon territorial areas, and deals with property as well as with persons through territorial relations (1877). This mode of interpretation practically leads anthropology to deprive a vast number of societies of politics. Morgan was the victim of his own theoretical system, which, in this case, was partly borrowed from Maine. He devoted several chapters of his great work to the 'idea of government' but he also denied the compatibility of the clan system (primitive society) with certain form of organization that are essentially political (aristocracy, monarchy). He also revived a controversy that is constantly recurring in anthropological theory. In 1956, Schapera returned to it once again in his book Government and Politics in Tribal Societies'.

Political Anthropologists

It was not until after 1920 that a different political anthropology, explicit and not implicit, was developed. It set not to study odd problems, but it used new material provided by ethnographical research. It revived discussion of the state, its origin and primitive manifestations – a question that had already been treated by Fraoz Oppenheimer in the early years of the century (Der Staat, 1907).

Within a few years of each other two important studies showing the same pre-occupation were published : The origin of the state was reconstructed in the light of the data of Aboriginal North America (1924) by W.C. Mac Leod, who uses evidence accumulated by American ethnographers, and the Origin of the State (1927) by R.H. Lowie, who determines the respective roles of internal factors (those responsible for social differentiation) and of external factors (those resulting from conquest) in the formation of states.

Both works were the result of approaches that claimed to be scientific, based on facts and sharply distinct from the intentions of political philosophy. The problem of origins was also considered by Sir James Frazer, who examined the relations between magic, religion and kinship and who became the initiator of the study of the relation between power and the sacred. In 1927, Beni Prasad published his THEORY OF GOVERNMENT IN INDIA. THE HISTORY OF POLITICAL THEORIES (1924) by A.A. Goldenweiser referred particularly to the political system of Iroquois of North America.

The first anthropological treatise paid little attention to political factors ; Frauz Boas devoted a chapter of his General Anthropology to the problems of government, while primitive society by Lowie systematized his theses and contributed a brief account of principal results. But the crucial anthropological revolution took place in the 1930s. The research devoted to segmentary societies (the so-called stateless societies), to the structures of kinship and the models of relationships that regulate these structures, lead to a better definition of the political field and a better understanding of its diversity.

It was in the field of American studies that the most rapid progress was accomplished. The societies investigated were organized on a larger scale, the differentiation of the relations of kinship and strictly political relations was expressed more clearly in the 'archaic' micro-socities. In 1940, three works were published that have since acquired classical status. Two of these, by E.E. Evans—Pritchard, contained the results of direct research and had new theoretical implications. The NUER, a book that presents the general features of a Nilotic Society, also reveals the relations and political institutions of a people apparently without government ; it shows that an 'ordered anarchy' can exist. THE POLITICAL SYSTEM OF ANUAK is exclusively a study in political anthropology and concerns a Sudanese people—neighbour of the Nuer—who have developed two contrasting and concurrent forms of human government. The third work, AFRICAN POLITICAL SYSTEMS, is a collection of essays edited by Evans—Pritchard and Meyer Forkes. By presenting a number of clearly differentiated 'cases', it has great value as a comparative study ; it is preceded by a theoretical introduction and offers the outline of a typology. Gluckman regards it as the first contribution in an attempt to give scientific status to political anthropology. Since 1945 there has been a rapid increase in the number of specialists in the field of African politics. Their studies are primarily the result of intensive field work. They examine both segmentry societies (Fortes, Middleton and Tait, Southall, Mercier, Apter. Beettie). They attempt to provide a theoretical framework and regional syntheses based on related systems. Tribes without rulers, published in 1958 under the editorship of Middleton and Tait, deals with lineage dominated societies. Primitive Government by Lucy Mair, published in 1962, concerns the states of the eastern interlacustrain region. Schapera's, GOVERNMENT AND POLITICS in Tribal Societies (1956) has, as its title suggests, a more general scope, though it is based entirely on examples from Southern Africa. It examines the mechanisms by which primitive governments function and elucidate certain problems of terminology.

Outside the Africant field, a single work dominates the specialized literature. Edmund Leach's political system of Highland Burma (1954) which is devoted to the political structures and organizations of the Kachin of Burma. The study gives particular prominence to the political aspect of social phenomenon. Following Nadel (and his predecessors) the society as a whole and the 'political unit' are identified, while the social structures are themselves examined from the point of view of 'ideas concerning the distribution of power between persons and groups of persons'. Leach develops—and this is his major contribution—a dynamic structuralism, with a wealth of suggestions most useful for political anthropology.

ECONOMIC ANTHROPOLOGY

Introduction

In modern world

Modes of Exchange

Barter

Ceremonial exchange

Reciprocity

Redistribution

Market

Trade—Market and Surplus

Bride wealth versus Bride price

Criticism

ECONOMIC ANTHROPOLOGY

Economic Anthropology may briefly be described as the study of that broad aspect of human activity concerned with the utilization of resources and the organization whereby they are brought into relation with human wants.

Introduction

At the technical conference in 1963, Eggan and Gluckman pointed out that technical economics has had less influence on social anthropological research than other social sciences have had. They offer the opinion that this is possibly because of the highly abstract nature of the economic discipline. Other factors have also been involved in the relative lack of development of economic anthropology.

The radical difference in the nature of the empirical phenomena has clearly been an impediment. The characteristic western institutional framework of business enterprise, with its machine technology, impersonal labour market, profit orientation, limited liability companies, international trading banking and credit, shows marked contrast to the small scale, highly personal, subsistence economic systems, with little in the nature of a market economy and perhaps even no money medium, with which anthropologists have traditionally been concerned. Small wonder that economists have tended to ignore these 'simpler' societies and most anthropologists have seen little in common between 'primitive' and 'civilized' versions of an economy. Even Karl Marx, with his structural interest in 'pre-capitalist formations' could find relatively 'primitive' material for his early studies and focussed attention primarily on Western and Oriental peasant and feudal or quasi-feudal systems. Again anthropologists have often been so concerned to demonstrate the contribution which economic behaviour makes to the maintenance of social systems that they have tended to take the economic phenomena for granted and to concentrate mainly on the social side of the equation.

The beginings of the study of economic anthropology can be traced far back in the nineteenth and even to the eighteenth century. But it is only about fifty years since Wilchelm Koppers (1915-16) and Màx Schmidt (1920-21) gleaned the material then existing from the works of Bucher, Cunow, Herment, Nohler, Lasch, Moszkowski, Santorius von Walters hansen, and other long forgotten writers, into synoptic and quasi-theoretical form. Following closely upon this came the more critical evaluation of Olivier Leroy (1925) and various combination of empirical inquiry and theoretical formulatlon by Richard Thurnwala, Bronislaw Malinowaski, W.E. Armstrong and Raymond Firth. Most prominent among later general works was that of Melville. Herskovits (1940) distinguished by its massive assemblage of fact and its robust common sense approach rather than by its command of economic theory over the last twenty years treatment of issues in economic anthropology has been more sophisticated, but threads of the discourse of those early years can still be discussed in the presentation and the controversies of today.

Economic Anthropology in Modern World

One of the major interests in economic anthropology has been descriptive—to find out how people in relatively simple technical conditions and with social fabrics very different from our own actually manage their economic affairs. Allied to this has been an interest of a more theoretical order to try to elucidate the principles that underlie such economic systems and their relation to a more general body of economic thought about the nature of society. In recent years, however, other trends of interest have also come to the fore. with the rapid development in technology and communications, large numbers of primitive and peasant communities have been brought into increasing contact with industrial economy and with new and powerful political and social forces. Social anthropologists have of necessity riveted their attention to the analysis of the changes taking place. Titles of studies such as FROM STONE TO STEEL OR MACHINE AGE MAYA epitomize a host of studies in this field.

Along side this development has grown an increasing interest in the study of concepts hitherto regarded as a primary concern of economists and economic historians. Among these is the notion of entrepreneur. Earlier anthropological studies could see little use to be made of this concept. But as C.S. Belshaw has pointed out (1955—p. 146) there are several ways in which anthropologists may legitimately interest themselves in the study of entrepreneurs. They may assess the function of enterprise in the economies of primitive or peasant peoples, and examine the ways in which leadership embodies enterprise and is reflected in organization. With the growing modern pre-occupation with processes of social change and problems of economic growth, anthropologist may study entrepreneurs as persons involved in these processes. Further, though it is as yet a relative uncharted area for our study, anthropologists may deal with the complex problems of modern business administration as an aspect of the working of small groups, more or less integrated with cultural elements external to the firm. Reviewing the various meanings of the term entrepreneur, as indicated by L.M. Fraser (1937) Belshaw points out that from the point of view of an anthropologist interested in social change, extensive management is more important than innovation in the function of an entrepreneur. An important feature of the anthropological analysis is the study of entrepreneurs as they fulfil social roles in relation with other elements of the society. Studies by Scarlett Epstein, Salisbury and Pospisil have added to our knowledge of entrepreneurship in societies of relatively simple technology, while Fredrik Barth and his collaborators (1964) have analysed entrepreneurship in complex European conditions.

In line with this general anthropological interest in the characteristics of entrepreneurs has been an increased concern with processes of choice and decision-making—a trend visible in other aspects of social anthropology as well. Here the economic anthropologist does two things : reveals empirically just what factors, in what combination, enter into situations of choice ; and indicates along what lines resolution of the choice is most commonly effected. Such analysis of actual processes of decision-making by Sutti Ortiz (pp. 191-226) yields results of interest to economists as well as to anthropologists.

It is from the point of view of the significance of what Lorraine Basic has termed the social variables, perhaps more than any other, that studies in economic anthropology can be significant in the applied field. Economic planners, for instance, not infrequently lack in the knowledge of the structure and norms of the community for which they plan. Here the provision of knowledge by anthropologists may be a very important component of the development process—though so far as a rule such provision has been conspicuously absent.

Justification for the study of economic anthropology does not have to be found only in its possible contribution to the solution of problems of economic growth. One can defend in pursuit of 'pure' knowledge even if not as an end in itself at least as essential for the proper development of an intellectual discipline and ultimately for the proper development of human personality. But even if one rejects utilitarian criteria as the index of worth one must recognise, as economists have already done, that to direct intellectual exploration towards the analysis of some concrete practical problem can give a powerful stimulus to abstract theoretical inquiry.

Two major sets of problems above all comfort anthropologist and economist alike in this developing situation. One set of problems relates to economic viability. As modernization advances and the full range of consumption goods and services of industrial society tends to be presented before the people of even the most remote underdeveloped areas of the world, these people will need to make a radical redeployment of their resources specially their labour resources if they are going to attempt to achieve the consumption levels which almost certainly they are going to demand. Traditional economic system are changing with almost explosive force, but it is not at all clear that such changes will be effective in securing the new wants. Hence another set of problems relates to the possibility of radical realignment of existing systems of control of resources and economic choices. Enough examples are available of such redeployment and realignment in recent history of African and Asian societies as to indicate a range of possible alternatives. But the analysis of the processes involved offers a challenge of great interest and importance to economic anthropology. Economists and Sociologists deal in generalizations, whereas anthropologists and historians deal with particular cases.

Modes of Exchange

In modern civilized communities, distribution is largely effected through money which thereby becomes a means of giving a numerical value to items of wealth. In some primitive communities there are established currencies which fulfil some of the functions of money. These should be described and indications be given of their measure of goods and services (measures of value). Elsewhere these conditions do not hold good, but there are nevertheless certain forms of exchange by periodic exchange of goods and/or services. One role of exchange is in facilitating the productive process by allowing the factors of production to receive their reward in goods other than the object produced. Another role of exchange is in supplementing the resources of the community. It is usually of advantage to make a distinction between "internal" and "external" trade. The former includes not only the mechanisms of gift-exchange and barter between members of small, closely organised groups, notably kinship groups and village communities, but also exchange with a money medium in local markets.

Barter

Barter consists in the direct transfer of goods against goods. Unlike the gift exchange, it implies agreement as resarads the rates, with the possibility of haggling over quantities and values. A system of barter in certain communities may co-exist with gift exchange as in the Trobriands, where as described by Dr. Bronislaw Malinowaski, the Kulu or exchange of valuable armshells and necklaces is conducted along polite, strictly ceremonial lines while the GIMWALI, the barter of fish for vegetables, is carried on with haggling as to size and quantity and even acrimonious wrangling. Barter in abstract from is often supposed to be typical of primitive peoples. But very rarely in any native community is the rate of exchange for goods determined by purely economic considerations of supply and demand working on the principle of national utility alone.

Occasions of large scale trading activities among primitive peoples are provided by expeditions and markets.

Ceremonial Exchange or Custom of Gift

The analysis by Mauss, Marcel (Gift, 1954, London; Cohen and West) general had a profound and the most stimulating influence upon anthropologists. Stirred by Malinowaski's presentation of the Kula theme Mauss intended his theory to apply comparatively to the whole range of 'primitive' or 'archaic' types of society. It is relevant, then to see how far his conclusions are borne out when one considers societies other than those from which he has drawn material. Firth (1965, p. 331) fully bears out Mauss's emphasis upon the triple significance of the obligation to give, the obligation to receive and the obligation to repay. His insistence that every gift demands a counter-gift is illustrated by the fact that even when Tikopia state that an object is given SORIMORIFUERE—simply as a present—this does not mean that they necessarily have ruled out the wish or the obligation for a return. The distinction between this and TAUVI—'a payment is that the latter expresses a direct, overt exchange with equivalents agreed in advance, not exchanges which may be indirect and covert while reciprocity for a present may be long delayed, and is primarily at the discretion of the initial recipient, payment in overt exchange is usually expected to be immediate and on the agreed terms.

Ethnographically, however, Mauss's account of the process of gift making and return needs qualification. He cites POLYNESIAN material in support of his views that gift exchange takes place between groups in the form of 'total presentations' (1954) and refers his triple scheme of obligation primarily to such group relations. (though this is often overlooked by those who use his analysis). Now in Tikopia, a Polynesian society, gift exchange takes place between individuals as well as between groups. It would be contrary to the facts to state that in Tikopia it is groups not inviduals which carry on exchange, make contracts and are bound by obligations. Often gifts, with all the accompanying transactions, are made by chiefs or other elders and heads of social groups, but on many other occasions individual act upon their own responsibility and are not representative of a social unit. Again the term 'total presentation' is often implicable to Tikopia transactions(Sahlins 1965, 177) single items of objects or services are contributed and involve single items in return. These may be caught up in an elaborate system of gift and counter-gift but this does not necessarily involve in each case an exchange of the whole range of other social items included in the notion of 'total presentation'. In Tikopia Firth found no trace of the idea such as Mauss describes of the obligation to repay being based upod a belief that the thing initially given is not inert but embodies some part of the original owner's personality which afflicts the recipient if he does not repay the gift. In so far as the Tikopia believe in the possibility of a ritual sanction for repayment, it lies in the concept of a personal mobilization of spirit forces, an energised reaction on the part of the original owner invoking 'Sorcery', upon a recalcitrant debtor. But such ritual saction would seem to be rare. With the Tikopia, the sanctions for reciprocity lie primarily in the field of economic, social and moral aititudes.

Basically, the sanctions noted by Malinowaski, Mauss and other writers concerned to explain the widespread custom of the gift fall into three major categories : sanctions of economic and political advantage, sanctions of social status and sanction of ritual and religious belief. The obligations to give is based primarily upon sanctions of economic and political advantage and sanctions of social status, though in gifts made as a charity religions sanction is very important. Economic and political sanctions appear with varying clarity in different types of transaction. Malinowaski stressed the importance of the principle of reciprocity and conceded that even this category of free gift could be reinterpreted in terms of return for services. Mauss too emphasises the importance of the social sanction in the obligation to give, though he discusses this primarily in reference to the potlatch, and implies that the sanction of prestige—of losing 'face' is as much institutionalised as personal in its effect.

Reciprocity

Labour, natural resources and products are transacted by any of three socio-economic rules or principles—reciprocity, redistribution and market exchange (Polanyi-1957).

Reciprocity is obligatory gift and counter gift giving between persons who stand in some socially defined relationship to each other. Indigenously, gifts of produced items and factors are regarded simply as one form—material or economic—of expressing such social relationship (In Western society, a birth day gift from father to son is just one among many ways of expressing their kinship relation).

Reciprocity plays a much more important part in primitive economies than in our own : the frequency and relative amount of such gifts are greater ; the number of different people with whom one person may engage in gift exchange is larger ; the social obligations (and sanctions) to so are stronger ; and, above all, such gift reciprocity may play an important part in production (specially in labour allocation), which is rarely the case in our own economy outside the family farm.

After describing the network of obligatory gift transfers of labour and material products among kins and friends, at normal times as well as during festive occasions. Schapera and Goodwin explain the importance of reciprocal flows in Bantu societies :

The main incentive to conformity with these obligations is reciprocity. In the relative absence of industrial specialization and consequent economic interdependence, kinship serves to establish greater social cohesion within the community, and to integrate its activities into a wider co-operation than obtains within the restricted limits of the household. The so-called "communal system" of the Bantu is largely a manifestation of this close bond of solidarity and reciprocity arising out of kinship and affecting well-nigh every aspect of daily life (1937 : 166).

The great variety of items and services transacted reciprocally with the same set of persons helps to explain why "production" is not a distinct activity (as it is with us), separate it from other activities, in primitive economies : from the viewpoint of the participants, the movement of resources and products is one of many social activities. There are gifts of labour to help a kinsman clear his land (part of production), gifts of cattle to help him acquire a bride, gifts of a song or a name, and reciprocal gifts to be expected from him when the need arises. The pivotal matter is the social relationship between the persons which induces gifts of labour, cattle, song and names when the source of the gift obligation is the same, there is no reason for the participants to mark off the labour gift as part of production. IT IS ONLY WHEN PRODUCTION ACTIVITIES BECOME DIVORCED FROM ACTIVITIES expressing social relationship and obligations that production becomes marked off as a peculiarly Economic activity apart from other activities (as, of course, occurs in market economy). With us, the place of production (factory, office etc) and the set of people we work with in production activities are usually different from the place where and the people with whom we live our family, religious, political and social lives. Few of us live over the store in a family enterprise.

Redistribution

Redistribution entails obligatory payments of material items, money objects, or labour services to some socially recognised centre, usually king, chief or priest who reallocates portions of what he receives to provide community services (such as defence or feasts) and to reward specific persons. Typically, but not invariably, the central figure, is also endowed with the right to distribute unused land or hunting sites, these allocation rights are vested in him in the name of the community by virtue of his high politicial, judical, military or religious authority. As with reciprocity between friends or kins, the obligations are multiple, economic and non-economic. One pays in labour, to lay the chief's garden or build his new house and one pays in respect, homage and political followership. Indeed what appear to us as economic transactions of resources and products need not be distinguished indigenously from such as express the obligation to perform military service.

Among the Bantus, chief receives the payments of specific goods and services from all his people and payments of fines and bride wealth. Such tribute payments are partly in recognition of his position as the steward of tribal land holdings and of his judicial authority. The word "tribute" is important here in both its economic and social meanings : the goods and labour paid over are tribute and the social recognition of authority signified by the payment is a tribute.

By virtue of his official status as head of the tribe he also played an important part in the economic organisation. He received tribute from his people, both in kind and in labour. He was given a portion of every animal slaughtered or killed in the Chase ; the LOBOLA (bride wealth) for his chief wife was paid by the members of his tribe ; he had the right to call upon his subjects to perform certain tasks for him, such as building his huts or clearing the land for his wives' gardens ; above all he received fees for hearing cases and fines for misdemeanours and in cases of homicide the culprit paid compensation not to the relatives of the deceased but to him (Schapera, 1928, p. 175).

His material receipts cannot be regarded apart from the chief's material obligation to his people. He uses the payments and fines for his own maintenance, but also to provide community services and to reward special service of his subjects ; he also gives hospitality and provides emergency support to the afflicted.

All this accumulation of wealth by the chief was really made on behalf of the tribe. One quality which was always required of the chief was that he should be generous. He had to provide for the members of his tribe in times of necessity. If a man's crops failed he would look to the chief for assistance ; the chief gave out his cattle to the poor members of his tribe to have for him, and allowed them to use the milk ; he rewarded the services of his warriors by gifts of cattle ; his subjects frequently visited him in kis kroal and during their stay he fed and entertained them (Schapera, 1921, p. 175).

Just as an individual receives land from his chief and labour from his wives, and frieds as a matter of right, so too, does he receive material and in time of need as a matter of social right. Subsistence is guaranteed among the Bantu—as is the case widely prevalent in primitive Africa—in the ways : through socially structured rights to receive land and labour and through emergency allotments of food from the chief and gifts from kin. It is these socially assumed rights to labour, land and emergency subsistence which have sometimes been mistaken for "primitive communism".

Market

The market place is a specific site where a group of buyers and a group of sellers meet. The market mechanism, network or market principle on the other hand entails the determination of prices of labours, resources and outputs by the forces o supply and demand, regardless of the site of transactions. The market principle often operates outside the market place asf when a business firm hires labor, land is sold in the real estate market, or grain is sold in the world market. When most of the anthropologists use the term "markets" they mean market places and not the diffuse interaction of suppliers and demanders through a network of integrated resource and product markets such as in U.S. economy. The two, of course overlap in many, but by no means all, instances.

The three typical situations can be summarized as follows :

1. Communities which lack market places and in which the market principle is but weakly represented.
2. Community with petty markets—that is the institution of market place is present but the market principle does not determine acquisition of subsistence or the allocation of land and labour resources.
3. Communities dominated by labour, resource and product, markets and the price mechanism, but usually retaining simple technology and traditional culture that is underdeveloped peasant economies.

Trade—Market and Surplus

The word "trade" is commonly used to mean several activities :

1. any commercial transaction ;
2. activities of professional specialists ; and
3. any external transaction (foreign trade)

The first two uses of the word "trade" distinguish two kind of action. There is on the one hand, selling one's own produce and buying one's needs, which we shall call "marketing". On the other hand, there is buying in order to resell. The French term COMMERCER expresses precisely this latter meaning—that of professional trading. Most anthropologists express the same idea by the terms "middlemen". The market and "cemmercize" are not the same thing, and in Africa they are sometimes institutionally separated selling a minor portion of produce can be an integral part of subsistence farming. Buying for resale is an additional activity.

External trade has special aspects that distinguish it from marketing and professional trading. In Africa much external trade was an activity of state—"administered trade" to use Polanyi's term primarily in prestige or treasure items of elite circulation. The market principle was not the mode of transacting, nor typically, was the market place the site of such transactions.

It has frequently been said that marketing byuing for resale or extetnal trade arises from surpluses. Too often the terme "surplus" is used to mean simply that which is sold or exchanged.

A special of external trade was induced by the exact opposite of surplus, namely an emergency shortage in which prestige, items (including slaves, children and women) were traded off for subsistence goods. Examples of such emergency conversions are found among Guro, Kipsigis. It was rather that goods moved between people of pre-eminent status on customary terms, until they reached the upper part of the country, whereupon they traded at terms of exchange which profited the upper Guno.

Bride Wealth versus Bride Price

The controversy over "bride wealth" versus "bride price" (Gray 1960 ; Gulliver 1961 ; Gibson 1962) is a symptom of theoretical malaise that afflicts economic anthropology like controversies over whether sea shells and dog's teeth are really money (Dalton, 1965). The issue comes down to this : on what grounds is it useful to employ a term with a very special meaning in developed capitalist economy—price—to describe a transaction in primitive economy that in some ways resembles the price transaction in our own and in some ways does not ? The issue is not merely terminological. To use the term "bride price" is to imply that payment at marriage is a market or commercial transaction and therefore that marriage entails a commercial purchase of rights or service.

Evans-Pritchard's Position

The term "bride price" is mlsleading because "price" has an inseparable association with the commercial transaction of market purchase in European Economy. The material goods and services that form a necessary payment at marriage—bride wealth—are not the same as the dollar price of a commodity (1) the participants do not regard the payment of bride wealth as a commercial transaction (although it does have an "economic" component in the sense that material goods and services enter) and (2) from the view point of the anthropologist, the social situation of which bride wealth is a part marks off the transaction sharply from impersonal market purchase. The events and circumstances of bride wealth are different in important ways from those of a commercial exchange.

These are very good reasons for cutting the term (bride-price) out of ethnological literature since at best it emphasizes only one of the functions of this wealth, an economic one, to the exclusion of other important social functions and since at worst it encourages the lay man to think that "price" used in this context is synonymous with "purchase" in common English parlance. Hence we find people believing that wives are brought and sold in Africa in much the same manner as commodities are bought and sold in European markets (Evans-Pritchard, 1931, p. 36).

Bride wealth paid at marriage has different functions in different societies and may have served in the same society : to indemnify the girls family for the loss of her services as an earnest of good intentions on the part of the groom and his family to solidify the new affinial bonds created by marriage, and to legitimize children born to the union and affiliate them in the socially approved manner. It is better therefore to use a neutral term, one that does not single out one of these functions, the economic" as the most important.

I do not myself see the necessity of using a symbol which refers to any one particular function of this wealth as is the case with "price", "earnest" and "indemnity" but propose instead the term "bride wealth" because it does not attempt to define what are the many aspects of this transference of wealth in the situation of marriage . . . the term bride wealth stresses very definitely the economic value of all the different things which are handed over by the group of a man to the group of a woman as one of the concrete obligations of the union. For whatever else they may be cattle, spears, goats, arrows, pots, labor etc. have an economic value. But while the economic value of these things is suggested in term "bride wealth" there is no expressed indication that the wealth has any one particular economic function such as implied in the word "price", a function which is as a matter of fact, very little developed among African peoples out of contact with Europeans (Evans—Pritchard, 1931 : 38).

Gray's Position

Among the Soujo, transactions involving marriage payments are much like other transactions (such as those involving rights to irrigation water) because the same item—goats—is used to make payment. Therefore it is useful to emphasise the similarity between payments at marriage and other transactions by treating bride price also as an economic transaction (just as we regard the exchange of irrigation rights for goats as economic). Indeed the economic terms such as "purchase", "sale" and "price" if properly redefined, can be applied to point out the similarity between bride price payments and other transactions in the Soujo community.

The real question at issue is not, as Evans Pritchard's statements suggests, whether African wives are bought and sold in the same manner as commodities are bought and sold in European markets : it is whether women in some African societies are transferred as wives in a manner that has a basic resemblance, to the manner in which others economic commodities are transferred in the same societies. Where this resemblance is found, and economic terms are applied to dealings in other commodities, I shall argue that it is legitimate to apply them to dealings in wives as well (Gray 1960 : 35).

Criticism

The ambiguity in Gray's argument is due to his implicit use of the word "economic" to mean "commercial" so that all exchanges of "economic commodities" in Soujoland are transmogrified into market exchanges. If goats paid for irrigation rights are economic (commercial) then goats paid for bride are economic (commercial) too. Therefore we may call marriage payments "bride price". But markets do not exist in Soujoland, so he must refine market terms (purchase, sale price) to make them include any kind of exchange, whether it be reciprocal gift giving, redistributive payments to central authority or commercial purchase.

But this is precisely what one should not do if there are essential differences between market and Soujo exchanges. To redefine familiar terms in order to homogenize transactions does not solve the problem as long as the Soujo exchanges are essentially different from the Market exchanges in our own economy to which these terms apply. To call a cat quadruped and then to say, because cats and dogs are both quadruped so call them all cats, does not change the nature of cats. Naither does it confuse dogs, it merely confuses the reader. To say that Soujo women are commodities purchased and sold at a price is to say that they are transacted like shoe polish in car economy. They are not. It is confusing to use the same words for different types of transactions and by so doing some points of analytical interest about Soujo economy are obscured.

In sum what led Gray to prefer the term "bride price" is that the items comprising the marriage payment—goats—are also used in other Soujo exchanges. And if these other transactions are "economic" so, too, in the marriage transaction. In Gray's context, "economic" should mean simply a commercial or market exchange (Dalton 1961 : 5-7). In American Society, too marriage has an "economic" component—material goods such as wedding rings and presents are involved—but this does not mean that we interpret marriage as the groom buying the bride with a wedding ring or gifts to her parents. Gray errs in using the word "economic" to mean "commercial" instead of simply "goods and services".